PRAISE FOR *WHAT KEE*

These pages glisten with hope for the paralyzed heart trying to pursue their God-given dreams. My friend, Pete, will help you see there is a quest with your name on it. And even better, he'll help you boldly trust God as you see those dreams turn into reality.

—LYSA TERKEURST, *NEW YORK TIMES*
BESTSELLING AUTHOR OF *THE BEST YES* AND
PRESIDENT OF PROVERBS 31 MINISTRIES

If you are unsure about the future and find yourself paralyzed with fear, this book will set you on the path toward God's best for your life. You don't need to give in to fear or sit on the sidelines of life. Even in the midst of uncertainty, read this book and discover how God can help you become all that you were created to be.

—STEVEN FURTICK, LEAD PASTOR OF ELEVATION
CHURCH AND *NEW YORK TIMES* BESTSELLING
AUTHOR OF *CRASH THE CHATTERBOX*,
GREATER, AND *SUN STAND STILL*

Sometimes, I get up early to hustle on my dream. Other nights, stress kicks me out of the bed and anxiety chases me into the day. If you've ever felt that way, don't skip this book. We all face uncertainty, but we're not meant to face it alone and Pete's new book is a powerful reminder of that!

—JON ACUFF, *NEW YORK TIMES* BESTSELLING
AUTHOR OF *DO OVER*, *START*, AND *STUFF*
CHRISTIANS LIKE

Pete's teaching has had an immense impact on my life. He has a unique gift to help you overcome obstacles that are keeping you from experiencing the peace and confidence only God can give. I'm someone who is prone to struggle with anxiety, and this book is helping me fall asleep with a deeper sense of rest and encouragement for the journey ahead. I believe it will do the same for you.

—NATALIE GRANT, GOSPEL MUSIC'S 5-TIME
FEMALE ARTIST OF THE YEAR

What Keeps You Up at Night? is a grand-slam home run! Pete Wilson writes with such insight and humor, but always with an eye to real-life situations. He offers a powerful challenge to trust God in every situation and to keep chasing your dreams. You will love this book!

—JUD WILHITE, AUTHOR OF *PURSUED* AND
SENIOR PASTOR OF CENTRAL CHRISTIAN
CHURCH

Pete Wilson has a keen mind, an open heart, and a winsome voice. In this book he stands at the crossroads marked "Hope" and "Fear" and points the way with wisdom. I hope what keeps you up at night is reading *What Keeps You Up at Night?*!

—JOHN ORTBERG, SENIOR PASTOR OF MENLO
PARK PRESBYTERIAN CHURCH AND AUTHOR
OF *SOUL KEEPING*

All of us have felt overwhelmed, anxious, or without passion at some point in our lives. God can restore your confidence in and passion for a relationship with Him. That's what Pete's new book *What Keeps You Up at Night?* is all about. Pete tells real stories and provides practical advice to walk in confidence and trust that the best is yet to come. I would highly recommend it to anyone looking to figure out how to trust God and what He has next for your life!

—MARK BATTERSON, *NEW YORK TIMES*
BESTSELLING AUTHOR OF *THE CIRCLE MAKER*

Pete is one of the most authentic guys I know, and his sincerity shines through in *What Keeps You Up at Night?* He opens up about some tough times in his own life to show you how to keep fear and uncertainty from ruining the plans God has for you. If you've ever been scared and confused about what to do next, this is the book for you.

—DAVE RAMSEY, *NEW YORK TIMES*
BESTSELLING AUTHOR AND NATIONALLY
SYNDICATED RADIO SHOW HOST

At the threshold of every major transition in your life you will be confronted by fear. In order to fulfill your purpose you must be strong, courageous, and boldly take some risks. We only have one life to live, and nothing of any lasting value has even been achieved behind the walls of comfort, safety, or security. *What Keeps You Up at Night?* will help you to not only discover the adventure you were born to live, but to actually live it.

—CHRISTINE CAINE, FOUNDER OF THE A21
CAMPAIGN

I know I'm not the only one who has battled through a difficult season of depression and anxiety. What I can tell you is this: Jesus has the power to lead you through this until the end. You CAN walk in confidence, you CAN trust that the best is yet to come, and you CAN grow closer to Jesus than you've ever been before. It will take time, but you CAN get there. That's what Pete's book *What Keeps You Up at Night?* is all about. If you're overwhelmed, looking to find your passion again, or just trying to find relief from some of the anxiety you're feeling, I highly recommend reading this book!

—PERRY NOBLE, SENIOR PASTOR AT
NEWSPRING CHURCH AND AUTHOR OF
UNLEASH! AND *OVERWHELMED*

WHAT KEEPS YOU UP AT
NIGHT?

WHAT KEEPS YOU UP AT
NIGHT?

HOW TO FIND
PEACE WHILE CHASING
YOUR DREAMS

PETE WILSON

W Publishing Group

An Imprint of Thomas Nelson

Published in Nashville, Tennessee, by W Publishing Group, an imprint of Thomas Nelson.

Pete Wilson is represented by The Litton Group, a brand management and content strategy agency in Brentwood, Tennessee. Learn more at www.TheLittonGroup.com.

Thomas Nelson titles may be purchased in bulk for educational, business, fundraising, or sales promotional use. For information, please e-mail SpecialMarkets@ThomasNelson.com.

Unless otherwise noted, Scripture quotations are taken from the Holy Bible, New International Version®, NIV®. © 1973, 1978, 1984, 2011 by Biblica, Inc.™ Used by permission of Zondervan. All rights reserved worldwide. www.zondervan.com.

Scripture quotations marked NLT are taken from the *Holy Bible*, New Living Translation. © 1996. Used by permission of Tyndale House Publishers, Inc., Wheaton, Illinois 60189. All rights reserved.

Scripture quotations marked KJV are taken from the King James Version of the Bible. Public Domain.

Library of Congress Cataloging-in-Publication
Data Available Upon Request

ISBN: 978-0-8499-6457-2

Printed in the United States of America

15 16 17 18 19 RRD 5 4 3 2 1

To Mom and Dad,
It's impossible to thank you adequately for everything
you've done, from loving me unconditionally to teaching
me that anything is possible for those who believe, to
allowing me to follow my dreams. I obviously didn't
fully appreciate or acknowledge how difficult it is to be
a parent until I became one myself. You guys continue
to do it with grace and class and I'll be forever grateful.

"This is my command—be strong and courageous!
Do not be afraid or discouraged. For the Lord
your God is with you wherever you go."

—Joshua 1:9 NLT

CONTENTS

INTRODUCTION

SEEING CLEARLY

"Vision is the art of seeing what is invisible to others."
—Jonathan Swift

There's a powerful scene in one of C. S. Lewis's classic stories from the *Chronicles of Narnia*. It happens in *The Voyage of the Dawn Treader,* which tells the story of Prince Caspian's voyage into the distant reaches of the Great Eastern Ocean in search of the Lost Lords of Narnia. One day, they approach what appears to be an island of mist, floating on the sea. They soon realize it is not a mist at all, but pure darkness. Moving a little way into it, they hear cries for help. Soon they pull from the water a terrified swimmer who has been marooned on the dark island. His face filled with terror, he tells them that the darkness contains the Island where Dreams Come True.

At first, the crew of the *Dawn Treader* thinks the man

must be confused. Who wouldn't want to live forever in the place where one's fondest dreams become reality? But he quickly gives them the chilling explanation: he isn't talking about wishes or daydreams. He's talking about nightmares—about their worst, darkest fears. In a heartbeat, every hand on board is rowing madly, trying to escape the darkness. As they go, each of them is grappling with the terrifying sensation that his or her secret horror is about to begin.

What keeps you up at night? What is *your* worst fear? Each of us has one. At some time or another, each of us must come to grips with the particular fear that tortures our sleep, that one event or circumstance that seems to have the power to rob our lives of all joy, all happiness, all hope.

Maybe for you, it's the fear of failure—especially the public variety. Or maybe you fear that your kids won't get on the right sports team or into the right school. We fear for our financial well-being. We fear for our health. We fear that our careers may never take off or that they may be brought to a sudden halt by a poor economy or by poor decisions. Maybe you're afraid your marriage won't make it or that your child will never come back to the faith you tried to instill in him or her. The reasons we fear are as many and varied as our experiences.

Trust me, I'm no different than anybody else. I'm afraid of being an ineffective husband or dad, of messing up a really important decision, of making a financial investment that goes south, of saying or doing something that scars my kids for life, of waking up one day and realizing I'm irrelevant, for the safety of friends who are serving God in a dangerous part of the world; afraid of the future; afraid of the unknown.

I fear.

And fear can inflict some ugly consequences on our lives. It is perhaps the world's most pernicious thief. It steals our joy in the present and robs us of our hope for the future. It causes us to obsess over ourselves and our limitations instead of seeing all the possibilities that are available. It keeps me from connecting with other people and prevents me from allowing myself to be vulnerable or trusting. It erodes my faith and confidence, preventing me from daring to do what God has called me to do in this world. It deceives me into crawling inside a box in an attempt to be safe when I was really created to take glorious risks in the wide-open air.

Fear is a dirty enemy; it doesn't fight fair. It finds our soft spots, our weak links, and mercilessly exploits them. It whispers lies in our ears at night and saps our strength in the morning.

Blinded by Fear?

This past summer I turned forty. I had been told for years that as I got older things would start to change. Metabolism would start to slow down or even crawl. I'd start to develop aches that I didn't have before.

However, the first change I started to notice was with my vision. My entire life I've had 20/20 vision, but all of a sudden I started struggling to see clearly. One day I couldn't read the teleprompter on a video shoot; the next thing I knew, I couldn't read street signs!

So, just the other day, I went to get my first eye exam. Part of the exam included a procedure my eye doctor called "dilating." He put some drops in my eyes, and for the next several hours I couldn't see a thing. Everything was blurry.

On my way home I tried to call my wife, and I couldn't even see the numbers on my phone while I was sitting in the parking lot (don't worry; I wasn't trying to drive!). Fortunately, over the next several hours, my sight started to slowly clear.

Similarly, when I am struggling with the gap between my expectations and my present reality, I have to remind myself that fear is a visual impairment. Most of us forget this, especially when we are in the grip of uncertainty, anxiety, or discouragement. Our vision gets skewed by our circumstances, and we start to see things inaccurately. Often, we see things that don't even exist!

I heard about a girl on one of her first church youth group trips, to the Guadalupe River in Texas. The group was going to go rafting, and one of the preparatory exercises involved going down a steep chute into the river. Without any explanation of what was about to happen, she said, the guides had them go down this chute, and when she hit the water at the bottom, she was tumbling back and forth, completely disoriented, trying desperately to claw her way to the surface. She remembers thinking, *All my friends are standing on the bank, and they're about to watch me drown.*

Then, somebody hollered at her, "Stand up!"

She was in about two feet of water. The problem was that—because of her disorientation, confusion, and *fear*—she was fighting a problem that didn't really exist!

Fear is disorienting. It can cause us to fight nonexistent enemies; it can cause us to focus on the wrong things. It creates problems with our vision.

One of the first casualties of our fear-induced vision problem is our image of ourselves. We think that something must be wrong with us. Otherwise, why would these obstacles be in our path?

This reminds me of the time when Jesus and His followers came upon a blind man. The poor fellow had been blind since the day of his birth; he had never witnessed the blue of the sky, the sparkle of sunlight on water, or the kind face of a friend. He lived in a world of perpetual darkness.

Jesus' followers assumed that somebody, somewhere, had messed up in order to cause the man to have such misfortune in his life. "Who sinned," they asked Jesus, "this man or his parents, that he was born blind?" (John 9:2).

Jesus explained to them that nobody had sinned. This man was a creation of God, and his circumstances would become an opportunity for God's goodness to be revealed.

That's the way it is with us when we encounter opposition or difficult circumstances. Like Jesus' followers, we assume that we are somehow defective or messed up. What else could explain all this trouble we're having?

But the truth is that every single person on the planet, at some point in life, struggles with fear. It is part and parcel of human life in the world we live in. No matter what your struggles may be, you are not unique or alone.

Your Best Ally

One of the devil's most successful tactics is isolation. If Satan can convince you that you are all alone with no help, he can twist your perception to make you believe almost anything he wants.

The good news is that God doesn't leave us alone to duke it out with our fear the best we can. No, God fights alongside us. Jesus walked among us as one of us, and He knows all about fear.

In fact, of the 125 direct commands or imperatives of Jesus recorded in Scripture, 21 of them have to do with over-coming fear. Over and over again, Jesus encourages us to "not be afraid" or "fear not" or "have courage" or "take heart." Take a few seconds to reflect on that. The single statement He made more than any other was "Don't be afraid." Jesus takes our fears quite seriously!

Listen, my friend. If there is a voice in your head telling you that you are the only one who is afraid, that you are somehow flawed in ways nobody else could possibly understand, that you are messed up and there is no point in trying anymore, trust me on a very basic fact: it is not God's voice you are hearing!

You are not alone! You do have help! You have a God who knows your fears and who will battle them on your behalf. You have a God who cares deeply and intimately about you and who has planted dreams in your soul that He longs to help you fulfill. All you need are God's spiritual corrective lenses so you can see clearly and realistically.

Changing Your Focus

One of my favorite scriptures is Psalm 121. It begins:

> I lift up my eyes to the mountains—
> where does my help come from?
> My help comes from the LORD,
> the Maker of heaven and earth.
> He will not let your foot slip—
> he who watches over you will not slumber.

I love these verses because they illustrate perfectly what it looks like when we are seeing clearly, seeing past our fear. They present an image of the confidence that comes when God, not our fears or difficulties, is at the center of our focus.

In Hebrew, the phrase "I lift up my eyes" carries the meaning of noticing and becoming part of something. It indicates peering intently, with purpose. That is how we get our vision corrected. We peer intently at God, purposefully becoming part of what God is doing in our lives.

This psalm captures in a few words one of our greatest freedoms as humans: the freedom to choose what we focus on. That is a choice nothing in heaven or earth can take from us. But we have to choose wisely.

You see, if I choose to, I can focus my attention on my problems. I can focus my attention on my fear, on my heightened sense of vulnerability, and my diminished sense of power. Or I can focus on God. I can do that anytime, anywhere.

The Illusion of Isolation

Someone once said that people are like icebergs; most of what we are is hidden below the surface. Nowhere is that more true than when thinking about the topic of fear and failure.

Consider this: In a typical day, how many of the people you interact with mention their greatest fear or something they're struggling with? I would guess the answer, at least for most of us, is "not many" or "none." (Now, I get it: that's not usually the case for me because I'm a pastor, which sort of gives people an open invitation to talk to me about the problems in their lives; but I think you get my point.)

Most of us try, to some extent, to present a brave face to the world. When we pass somebody in the hall at work and they ask, "How's it going?" we usually respond "Good, how about you?" If you strike up a conversation with somebody in the car pool or at a chance encounter at the mall, they'll most often leave you with the impression that everything is rolling along pretty smoothly. In fact, it requires rather dire circumstances for most of us to admit to anybody—pastor or not—that we are dealing with something bad or that we are fearful about the future.

This tendency often leads us to conclude, during our times of anxiety and difficulty, that we must be weird, messed up, or otherwise unusual. After all, everybody else is doing well—they told you so! But the fact is that many—if not most—of the people around you are keeping their own problems, fears, and anxieties hidden below the surface. We assume, based on our incomplete knowledge, that we are the only ones experiencing conflict or adversity.

It's kind of odd when you think about it. We've all got these huge gaps of information in our knowledge of what's really going on with the people around us every day. The difference is that when we think of other folks, we fill in the gaps with the most optimistic assessment, and when we think of our own situations, we fill in the gaps with worst-case scenarios. It's like we can have faith and confidence on behalf of others, but we can't have them on our own behalf!

Whatever is going on in your body, in your bank account, your marriage, your career, your kids' lives, or in any other part of your world, you can—right now—if you choose, focus on God. You can lift up your eyes and peer intently at Him. You can remember that your help comes from God—not from you, *from God*. And God is bigger than anything you are facing right now, no matter what it is.

There is help. You are not alone.

So, let's get started. Yes, this world can be a really scary place. But you can learn how to keep moving forward—even when you're scared to death.

How to Use This Book

I encourage you to think of this book as a field guide to ruthlessly trusting God's plan—even in the face of difficulty and uncertainty. Each chapter discusses some aspect of embracing God's call for your life, based on Scripture and my observations and experiences.

Through the years, I have seen God accomplish some breathtaking things in the lives of people who were willing to completely put their trust in Him, and I've tried to record in this book what I've learned, both on my own journey as well as observing and, in some cases, assisting with the journeys of others.

Each chapter contains helpful subheadings to act as guideposts, aiding you as you walk through the material. And at the end of each chapter, you'll find a list of key ideas—sound bites from the chapter that communicate the most important ideas covered. You'll also find a few reflection questions that will help you frame, for yourself and others, the key concepts or challenges associated with the chapter topics. These questions are particularly helpful if you're reading this book with a friend, spouse, or coworker. I believe that if it's at all possible, you're always better off reading this book—or any book, for that matter—with someone.

Finally, you'll see "Your Next Step." These are simple exercises or practical ideas you can put into action to get you moving in the direction of God's unfolding plan for your life. These can be a great way to give yourself the nudge you need to embrace life's inevitable uncertainties and step out in faith.

I invite you to turn the page—in this book and in your life—and begin to discover how God can help you become all you were created to be.

ONE

STEPS IN THE DARKNESS

*"But instead of spending our lives running
towards our dreams, we are often running away
from a fear of failure or a fear of criticism."*
—Eric Wright

Let me introduce you to some people I know. I won't use their real names, but you probably know some of them, too.

Adam, a fifty-three-year-old top executive at a prominent engineering firm, just found out that because of a slumping economy, his position—along with his high six-figure salary—is being eliminated. He had worked his way up from the bottom, and this was his dream job. He is wondering what he and his family will do now.

Carrie, a forty-two-year-old mother of three, just got a phone call from her gynecologist. As far as she knew, her last checkup was routine, but what she hears on the phone is anything but.

Tyrone, a thirty-six-year-old professional, was feeling exhilarated three days ago because of the fantastic date he had with Fran. He sensed chemistry between them and had started daring to believe that at long last he had found the soul mate he had been praying for all of his life. But he just got a text message from Fran, and now he knows why his last two phone calls went unanswered.

Amber, a twenty-five-year-old musician, has been waiting for weeks to hear back from the producer who requested her demo. She is starting to wonder if what she thought was her big break is just another dead end.

Have you met any of these folks? Or . . . are you one of them? What do you do when you are afraid your dreams may not happen? How do you move forward in a landscape that looks unfamiliar and even dangerous? Are your dreams over?

Let's face it: we live in uncertain times. When all the rules are changing, when everything you thought you knew is suddenly called into question, it seems impossible to live confidently, to keep believing. Your rational mind tells you to take the next step, but you have no idea what the next step should be.

And yet, I believe there is a way to keep going in the direction of your dreams, even when the landscape is shifting. I also believe that taking those steps, even in the midst of fear and uncertainty, is what helps you become all you were meant to be—all that God wants you to be. I believe there really is a way to keep moving forward, even when you are scared to death.

This is a book about overcoming the fears that seem to paralyze us over and over. Even more importantly, it's about the way God gets involved in our lives to help us fulfill our deepest purposes.

It doesn't matter what your dream is. Whether your life's aim is to find a cure for cancer, to take God's Word to a place that has never heard it, to operate your own car repair shop, or to bake the best cakes anyone in your town has ever tasted, the pursuit of that passion is a precious and holy thing. It will take you places you never would have gone otherwise. It is God's path of transformation into all you were meant to be.

But there's a problem. Many of us, especially these days, are too afraid to keep walking the path.

The Trouble with Dreams

Starting with *Cinderella* in 1950 and coming right up to the present with *Frozen*, the Walt Disney studios have spent considerable effort to convince us—at least temporarily—that if we believe enough in our dreams, they can come true. And it is a fact that the first step to make a dream come true is to have a dream in the first place.

Makes sense, right? Without dreams—aspirations, hopes, expectations—we would never know the joy that comes when a cherished desire is fulfilled. We would never experience the satisfaction of seeing a hard-fought goal become reality.

So why is it, then, that so many of us are afraid of our own hopes? In fact, many of us spend much of our lives actively avoiding our hopes, running in the opposite direction.

I believe it's because we are afraid, pure and simple—afraid of disappointment, dashed hopes, broken hearts. I mean, if you never want anything, you can't be disappointed when you don't get it. If you don't have the desire or expectation of a richer, more fulfilled life, you don't have to worry about that ache in your soul that comes from being denied the desires of your heart.

The trouble is, each one of us is hardwired for dreaming. That's right; we were made to be dreamers! The writer of Ecclesiastes, in the Old Testament, explains it by saying God has "set eternity in the human heart" (3:11). In other words, we were created to yearn for something better, something more. We can't help ourselves; we have to dream. And that's where our fear problem comes in.

What is fear, really? Usually, when we talk about fear, we mean the unpleasant emotion that comes with the feeling something or someone is a source of pain, danger, or an undesirable outcome.

Not all fear is bad. Our hunter-gatherer forebears learned quickly, for example, that when you see or hear a large predator, that voice in your head yelling, *Get away fast!* needs to be heeded. In that case, fear keeps you alive. It is a flashing light on the dashboard of life that says, "Pay attention, or you'll die!"

But for most of us nowadays, fear has a different meaning. It typically has less to do with preservation of life and limb and more to do with a heightened sense of vulnerability and a diminished sense of power. And these fears are not imaginary! Fear of failure, fear of being alone, fear of disapproval, fear of poverty, fear of illness, fears for the well-being of the people we love—all these are very real, very present challenges that everyone faces. All of us struggle with fear—every single one of us.

But I'm here to tell you that fear shouldn't get the last word. Fear should not deter us in the pursuit of the lives God has for us, nor should it paralyze us. The fact is that you were meant for so much more, as Switchfoot tells us in their song "Meant to Live." The dreams in your heart are no accident; they were put there by God.

Your Dream and God's Plan

God has always used dreamers to do the really big stuff. Take Jacob, in the Old Testament, for example. God first revealed himself to Jacob in a dream of angels going up and down a ladder to heaven. And you have to understand that at that time, Jacob was on the run from his older brother, Esau, whom he had just swindled out of his rightful inheritance as oldest son. Things were pretty hot at home, so Jacob's mother had sent her favorite son to her brother's house in Harran until Esau's rage cooled down. The Bible records what Jacob thought about the dream:

> When Jacob awoke from his sleep, he thought, "Surely the LORD is in this place, and I was not aware of it." He was afraid and said, "How awesome is this place! This is none other than the house of God; this is the gate of heaven. . . ."

Then Jacob made a vow, saying, "If God will be with me and will watch over me on this journey I am taking and will give me food to eat and clothes to wear so that I return safely to my father's household, then the LORD will be my God and this stone that I have set up as a pillar will be God's house, and of all that you give me I will give you a tenth." (Genesis 28:16–22)

Indeed, God had big plans for Jacob, despite what his angry older brother thought. Jacob would go on to become the father of twelve sons—who would in turn become the patriarchs of the twelve tribes of Israel. And—spoiler alert—he and Esau were eventually reconciled.

For a New Testament example, take a look at the apostle Paul. Throughout his career as a missionary, Paul received guidance, warning, and encouragement from his dreams. On one occasion, he was even permitted a peek into heaven itself (2 Corinthians 12:2–4). And trust me, if anyone could have used a glance past the pearly gates, it would be Paul. After all, this is the same guy who was falsely accused, beaten, shipwrecked, whipped, imprisoned—even bitten by a snake!

No Bed of Roses

The point is, there is overwhelming evidence that pursuing a God-given dream—whatever the dream may be—is guaranteed to bring you up against opposition. That opposition can come from many sources: naysayers and critics, well-meaning friends and family members, negative circumstances, and, most of all, from the fear in your own mind.

When we start facing disappointments, setbacks, bad news, or what have you, one of our first reactions is usually to say to ourselves something like this: *Hey, I thought I was doing God's will! What's the deal with all these trials and tribulations? God, how about a little support here? Whaddya say?* Our confidence in pursuing our passion is all too often overwhelmed by a riptide of fear and doubt.

Let me share this truth with you: the bigger the dream, the bigger the fight you'll face. In fact, the people throughout history who have been the most directly in the center of God's will for their lives are the same people who have gone through the toughest trials.

Think about it: Joseph, Moses, the prophets, Peter and the apostles, and of course, the best example of all, Jesus Christ Himself. There is a very good reason why the Messiah is described as a "man of sorrows, and acquainted with grief" (Isaiah 53:3 KJV).

So, it seems we can safely conclude that if we are expecting the universe to lavish approval on us for following our dreams, we are destined to disillusionment. Chasing a dream is no job for an approval junkie.

A Change in Perspective

Pursuing your passion will be accompanied by trials that will test your resolve to the utmost. The outcome of that testing is you will either grow stronger and more focused in your quest or you will be derailed.

I can promise you that, in my own life, I've gone off the rails more than once. As I look back on my journey, I can clearly see the times when fear, disappointment, and disapproval have taken over the driver's seat.

When I was just twenty-one years old I believed that God was prompting me to start a church. I thought it was kind of weird, but I simply couldn't shake this dream God had given me. At the time, I had been a youth pastor at a little country church about thirty miles away from the college I was attending. I had a few years of ministry experience but was realistically not prepared to start a church.

I remember sheepishly telling my pastor and boss at the time what I felt God was prompting me to do. Much to my surprise, he encouraged me to take whatever steps were necessary to follow God's will for my life.

A few weeks later I stood before the church and told them I was stepping down as the youth pastor to plant a new church. Everyone seemed tremendously supportive. I spent the next couple of weeks praying, planning, and getting ready for my leap of faith.

My last Sunday night on the job, the church I had been serving threw me a little party, mostly attended by the teenagers who had been a part of my youth group, along with many of their parents. We had a blast celebrating all that God had done the past few years in the life of those kids.

I stayed late helping clean things up, and eventually

everyone had left. I was walking out of the church, getting ready to lock it up for the last time, when I saw a light on in the church library. As I got closer I heard a couple voices in there. I recognized the voices of two deacons of the church. Just as I was walking by, I heard my name. I stopped out in the hallway and was shocked at what I heard next. These two deacons were going on and on about how they couldn't believe I was going to try to plant a church.

"Pete doesn't know how to plant a church."

"He doesn't have the resources."

"He doesn't have the experience."

"He doesn't know how to preach."

"He doesn't have any people."

"He doesn't even know where he's going to plant this church."

My heart sank. See, I knew everything they were saying was true, but I was still crushed. I felt fear instantaneously enter my veins and spread throughout my body. I attempted to hold it together long enough to run out to my car in the church parking lot. I got in the car and just started to sob. I remember praying out loud to God, "They're right. They're right. I don't have a clue what I'm doing, God. I don't know how to plant a church. I can't do this. It's going to be such a failure."

I continued to pray and confess every fear I had to God that night. Over the next few minutes I felt God impressing something deeply into my heart. I never heard a voice that night, but I sensed God saying to me, "Pete, you've got a huge decision to make. Are you going to listen to those men in there, or are you going to listen to me? Are you going to trust them, or are you going to trust me? Because here's the deal, Pete: for the rest of your life I'm going to prompt you to do things that will absolutely scare you to death. I'm going to prompt you to do things that won't always make sense to the people around you. Will you trust me?"

You know, that night I literally got out of my car and onto my knees in that church parking lot. I prayed and told God that to the best of my ability, the rest of my life I would trust in Him and be obedient to His prompts.

That night was a reminder to me that most of the time we don't really have a fear problem; we have a trust problem. When we focus on our fears, we stop focusing on God; we assume a position in the universe that we don't own. We stop trusting God and start trying to control things we can't control and manipulate circumstances we can't manipulate.

One of the things I hope to convince you of in this book is that the object is not learning to fear less; it's learning to trust God more. If your goal is to have a fear-free life, you'll never have a fear-free life. God is not a tool you can use for fear avoidance.

Let me say it this way: if you, your fears, or even your dreams are at the center of your story, things just aren't going to work out. But if God is at the center of your story—if, in fact, you can understand that God is *writing* your story—then you will be well on your way to becoming all that God intends for you to be, living your dreams in a way you could never have imagined.

Chapter One in Review

Key Ideas

1. There is a way to keep going in the direction of your dreams, even when the landscape is shifting. Taking those steps, even in the midst of fear and uncertainty, is what helps you become all that God wants you to be.
2. Many of us spend much of our lives actively avoiding our hopes because we are afraid of disappointment, dashed hopes, and broken hearts.
3. Pursuing a God-given dream—whatever the dream may be—is guaranteed to bring you up against opposition. The bigger the dream, the bigger the fight.
4. Most of the time, we don't really have a fear problem; we have a trust problem.

Reflection Questions

1. If you walked into your workplace tomorrow and one of the bosses said, "We're going to make some changes around here," what do you think your initial response would be?
2. In your opinion, what is the biggest obstacle for most people in following their dreams?
3. Think about the last time you were really afraid. What can you remember about your thoughts, words, and actions during that time?
4. Why do you think that those with the biggest dreams typically encounter the harshest opposition?

Your Next Step

Go to YouVersion.com, or a similar site, and do a search for the phrase "Do not be afraid" (if you prefer the King James Version of the Bible, you might use "fear not" instead). Notice how many times, in both the Old and New Testaments, God, an angel, or one of God's chosen leaders tells some person or group that they do not need to fear.

TWO

EXPECT CONFLICT

"Kites rise highest against the wind, not with it."
—Winston Churchill

I have done some checking with friends in the counseling business and have come to the following conclusion: no one ever comes in and requests counseling because everything is fine. For some unexplained reason, it seems that no one needs help dealing with positive circumstances. Seriously, in twenty years of ministry, I can count on one hand the number of times that people have scheduled a meeting with me just to let me know that things were going great in their life.

The truth is that none of us have any trouble handling life when things are going our way, right? Our default setting as humans seems to be "doing great!"

But we all know that those good times don't last. One

hundred percent of us will deal with difficulties, challenges, problems, and obstacles during our lives. Even Jesus Himself warns us, "In this world you will have trouble" (John 16:33). This is like Jesus' seven-day forecast for our life: trouble, trouble, trouble, trouble... "Get ready," He warns. "It's coming."

So why do tough times always seem to surprise us? Why is it that when we are walking through a season in the valleys of life, we wonder what is wrong, what we've done to deserve this, or why we've been singled out for such trouble?

The Whole Story

Never forget that you don't know the whole story about other people. Some of the most successful people you can imagine have also dealt with the most devastating failures you can imagine.

Take, for example, Michael Jordan. Here's a guy who is almost the personification of success when looking at his basketball career. After fifteen seasons in the NBA, he is hailed on the league's website as "the greatest basketball player of all time."[1] One of the most electrifying players on a Chicago Bulls team that won six NBA championships during his tenure, Jordan was named the league's MVP five times, was on the All-NBA First Team ten times, owns three All-Star Game MVP awards, ten scoring titles, three steals titles, and other honors. Although he retired from the NBA in 2003,

Jordan still holds the record for the highest regular-season scoring average and highest career play-off scoring average. In 1999, ESPN named him the greatest North American athlete of the twentieth century. He has been inducted into the Naismith Memorial Basketball Hall of Fame two times.[2] And don't even get me started about the success of his licensing and endorsement operations.

Yet here's how Jordan characterizes his career: "I've missed more than 9,000 shots in my career. I've lost almost 300 games. Twenty-six times, I've been trusted to take the game winning shot and missed. I've failed over and over and over again in my life. And that is why I succeed."[3]

Looking at Michael Jordan, would you have ever guessed that he failed so often? Most of us wouldn't.

Oprah Winfrey was sexually abused as a very young girl. She gave birth to a son when she was fourteen years old, and the child died soon after birth. She contemplated suicide. But she finished high school, was a debate champion, and was chosen as one of two high school students in Tennessee to attend a White House conference on youth. After graduating from college and getting her first job as a TV coanchor in Baltimore, Winfrey was fired, told she was "unfit for TV."[4] In 2013, Winfrey, by this time the head of a billion-dollar media empire, told the graduating class of Harvard that "failure is just life trying to move you in a different direction."[5]

One more story. Here's some text from a letter received by some hopeful young musicians back in 1979:

Dear Mr. Hewson:

Thank you for submitting your tape of "U2" to RSO. We have listened with careful consideration, but feel it is not suitable for us at present.

We wish you luck with your future career.

Yours sincerely,

Alexander Sinclair

RSO Records (U.K.) Limited[6]

In case you didn't already know it: "Mr. Hewson" refers to Paul David Hewson, the band's lead singer. You probably know him as Bono.

Now, the point I'm making is not tied to the celebrity or financial success of these examples. The main message here is that you cannot, simply by looking at people, conclude anything about the challenges they have faced in the past or are facing in the present. Remember, we're all like icebergs. We've all got troubles, even if nobody else can see them.

Meet Joseph

I love the story of Joseph, in the Old Testament, mainly because his story is so similar to the way we often experience life today. If you charted Joseph's circumstances on a line graph, it would look a lot like the Dow Jones Industrial Average over the last several decades: the overall trajectory was upward, but man, did Joseph's life take some serious downturns!

Joseph started out as the favored son of Jacob, a wealthy herdsman and farmer of Canaan, in what is now Israel. Joseph was a dreamer, in both the literal and figurative senses. Later in his life, his talent with dreams and their interpretations would come in very handy; but as a youngster still living at home, that talent nearly got him killed.

On one occasion, Joseph reported a dream he had in which he and his brothers were binding sheaves of grain. Suddenly, Joseph's sheaf stood upright, and the brothers' sheaves came and bowed down to it. You can imagine how well that went over. But Joseph didn't seem to get the message, because soon he had another dream in which the sun, the moon, and eleven stars were bowing down to him, and he not only shared *this* with his brothers, but with his father as well. Even Jacob was taken aback by his youngest son's audacity.

By this time, Joseph's brothers had a belly full of his grandiose dreams. One day, when they were a good distance from home, grazing their flocks, Jacob sent Joseph to check on them. They were plotting to kill him, but one of the brothers persuaded his siblings to toss Joseph into a dry cistern instead. Some traveling traders came along, and the brothers decided to sell Joseph to the traders.

The traders took Joseph with them to Egypt. They sold Joseph as a slave to an official in the Egyptian court, a man by the name of Potiphar.

But Joseph, the Bible tells us, had not been abandoned by God. In fact, Genesis 39 says:

The LORD was with Joseph so that he prospered.... When his master saw that the LORD was with him and that the LORD gave him success in everything he did ... Potiphar put him in charge of his household, and he entrusted to [Joseph's] care everything he owned. (vv. 2–4)

Potiphar benefited greatly because of Joseph's favor with God—so much so that the Bible tells us that before long, "with Joseph in charge, he did not concern himself with anything except the food he ate" (v. 6). These were good days at the headquarters of Potiphar, Inc. Profits were up, shareholders were happy, and life was easy.

But matters were about to take another downturn. You see, Joseph was a good-looking boy, and Potiphar's wife was apparently a lonely woman. Mrs. Potiphar soon began to make her desires known to Joseph. But Joseph remained loyal to his master: "My master has withheld nothing from me except you, because you are his wife. How then could I do such a wicked thing and sin against God?" (v. 9) he asked her.

As a poet once famously said, "Hell hath no fury like a woman scorned."[7] One day, Mrs. Potiphar grabbed Joseph and tried to have her way with him, but he pulled away, leaving part of his clothing in her hand as he ran out the door. She called in her other household servants and accused the young Hebrew of trying to rape her—and Joseph ended up in an Egyptian prison.

But once again the Bible reports that:

While Joseph was there in the prison, the LORD was with him; he showed him kindness and granted him favor in the eyes of the prison warden. So the warden put Joseph in charge of all those held in the prison. . . . The warden paid no attention to anything under Joseph's care, because the LORD was with Joseph. (Genesis 39:20–23)

The pattern is starting to sound familiar, isn't it?

Not long after Joseph becomes head trustee in the prison, Pharaoh's cupbearer and the royal baker are incarcerated because they have displeased Pharaoh. One night, both of these men have disturbing dreams.

Joseph knows that God, if He chooses, can make plain the meaning of the dreams, and he encourages the two officials to explain what they saw as they slept. They tell him, and Joseph gives them the meaning of their dreams.

In both cases, Joseph tells them their circumstances are going to change dramatically within three days. However, things are going to work out much better for the cupbearer than for the baker. The cupbearer will be restored to his position in Pharaoh's court, but the baker will be executed. I guess you can't win them all.

Events prove Joseph's interpretations accurate. Three days later, the cupbearer is back in Pharaoh's good graces, and the baker is dead. Joseph had asked the cupbearer to put in a good word for him when he returned to the palace, and as he watched the cupbearer being escorted out of the prison by the royal guards, he must have thought that his fortunes were about to regain an upward trend. He just needed this one break.

But Genesis 40:23 says, "The chief cupbearer, however, did

not remember Joseph." The cupbearer, no doubt dizzy with relief at being back on the job and not ending up like the baker, forgot all about Joseph. Joseph was stuck in prison—alone and forgotten. That is, until two years later, when Pharaoh had a dream of his own.

The king of Egypt had a night vision of seven fat cows and seven skinny cows; the skinny cows swallowed up the fat cows! Next, Pharaoh dreamed of seven healthy, full heads of grain and seven thin, drought-stricken heads, and once again, the poor specimens devoured the good ones.

The next day, the king started asking all his officials about the meaning of his dream. This caused the cupbearer to finally recall Joseph. Before long, Joseph was standing in front of Pharaoh, who asked him to give the meaning of the troubling dream.

I love Joseph's answer. "'I cannot do it,' Joseph replied to Pharaoh, 'but God will give Pharaoh the answer he desires'" (Genesis 41:16). Joseph explained to Pharaoh that God had sent him a message in his dreams. The seven fat cows and the seven healthy heads of grain symbolized seven years of good crops. But these would be followed by seven years of famine, symbolized by the skinny cows and the shriveled heads of grain.

Joseph advised Pharaoh to appoint someone of wisdom and discernment to go throughout Egypt and set aside a fifth of each of the next seven years' harvests, storing it up against the famine that was surely approaching. You can probably see where this is headed.

Pharaoh asked his officials, "Can we find anyone like

this man, one in whom is the spirit of God?" (Genesis 41:38). Therefore, as you've likely already guessed, he appointed Joseph as the second-in-command of all of Egypt and asked him to head up the brand-new National Famine Readiness Program.

As the famine tightened its grip in that part of the world, Joseph's father and brothers were feeling the pinch up in Canaan, along with everybody else. But Egypt had food to spare. So, Joseph's brothers headed south to see if they could buy enough grain to keep the wolf away from the door.

Imagine the emotions that must have coursed through Joseph as he saw his brothers come into the palace at Egypt. Just as in the dream that had gotten him in so much trouble many years earlier, here were the eleven, bowing down to this one they did not recognize as the brother they had sold into slavery.

Joseph messed with their heads a bit, but ultimately, there is a big family reunion as he brings his brothers, his father, and all their households down to Egypt to wait out the famine in comfort. And once again, I love what he says when he makes himself known to his brothers:

> Do not be distressed and do not be angry with yourselves for selling me here, because it was to save lives that God sent me ahead of you. For two years now there has been famine in the land, and for the next five years there will be no plowing and reaping. But God sent me ahead of you to preserve for you a remnant on earth and to save your lives by a great deliverance. So then, it was not you who sent me here, but God. (Genesis 45:5–8)

Later on, Joseph said to his brothers, "Don't be afraid. . . . You intended to harm me, but God intended it for good" (Genesis 50:19–20).

Joseph is seeing clearly! Despite all the ups and downs of his life, he can look back along the journey and realize that, all along, God had a plan. Even his misfortunes and suffering ultimately served the greater purpose of saving the lives of not only the people of Egypt but also his own family.

Clarity Comes Through Trust

That type of clear vision comes only with trusting God. And this brings up a point we will come back to several times in this book: Joseph's clarity was only in hindsight! When Joseph was lying at the bottom of the cistern, when he was trussed up on the back of one of the traders' camels, or even when he was imprisoned because of Mrs. Potiphar's accusations, I would bet that he had a hard time seeing anything positive on the horizon.

Only because Joseph was willing to keep on trusting God—despite his circumstances and despite the lack of all visible evidence of the possibility of a good outcome—was he able to reach the day when he could say to his brothers, "You meant it for harm, but God meant it for good."

Joseph's journey is, in many ways, a common journey. And it is certain that complete clarity only comes in retrospect and, even then, only after trusting God for all that we can't see.

There is a great story related by Brennan Manning

concerning Mother Teresa. He tells how the renowned ethicist, Jack Kavanaugh, journeyed to Calcutta to work with Mother Teresa in her ministry to the dying. When he got there, he asked her to pray for him.

She asked what he wanted her to pray for, and he said, "Clarity." But Mother Teresa refused. She made the wise observation that Kavanaugh was clinging to clarity and that he must release it. He questioned her, saying that she had always seemed to have tremendous clarity.

She laughed. "I have never had clarity. What I have had is trust. So I will pray that you trust God."[8]

Interesting, isn't it? I'd be willing to bet that some of you are praying for clarity these days.

God, how much longer is this going to go on?

God, when will things get better?

God, give me a sign of what we should do.

But, maybe you don't need more clarity. Maybe what you need is more trust.

Living with Faith in an Imperfect World

Now, the cynic might view this situation and ask, "What kind of God would toy with his creatures like that, exposing them to fear and conflict just so they can learn to rely on Him?"

My answer to that is God cares more about what we are becoming than He does about our circumstances. As Max Lucado has written:

God loves us right where we are, but he loves us too much to let us stay there.[9]

We are most often focused on what is happening *to* us, but God is more concerned about what is happening *in* us. In my own life I have to realize each day that there is a God . . . and I am not him. We can see this illustrated in the time Jesus spent with His disciples. Right up until the end of Jesus' life—and even for three days afterward—most of the disciples were convinced that Jesus was going to rally the nation of Israel to kick out the Romans and institute a new kingdom that would reestablish the Davidic monarchy. But that wasn't what Jesus was interested in, not what He came to do. What was so clear to the disciples was not even on Jesus' radar.

Everyday Courage

I sometimes think we've turned the life of faith into some kind of religious X Games. When we think of people of great faith, we think of Shadrach, Meshach, and Abednego in the fiery furnace, or Corrie ten Boom, who sheltered Jews and was ultimately imprisoned in the concentration camps during World War II; or maybe we even think of someone we're acquainted with who has made a radical life change in order to enter a mission field or work in inner-city ministry.

As inspiring and even intimidating as these examples are, I think we need to remember that God can also use acts of everyday courage and day-to-day faith. He honors the person who decides to love someone who others find unlovable. He exalts the individual who commits to being honest, no matter the personal consequences. He loves those who trust Him with their finances, even when things are tight and the future is unclear. He takes joy in the single mom who goes to one more job interview, even though she's already heard "no" over and over again, because she is determined to improve her situation in life. These, too, are acts of faith that delight the heart of our Creator.

"But," someone may ask, "How do you know when you're supposed to keep hanging on and when you're supposed to give up and move on to something else?"

That's a legitimate question, and I can't give an absolute, one-size-fits-all answer. I will suggest, though, that based on my observation, most of us give up too easily and too early. So, my bias would be on the side of persevering, rather than throwing in the towel.

My other comment is that, as a pastor and advisor, it is not usually my job to help you figure out your limits or to define your reality. Instead, I believe it is more often my task to help you see all the possibilities God is placing before you.

One of those possibilities is considering all that God may be doing in you and through you, even in the midst of your struggle and uncertainty. Yes, you are facing uncertain times, but is it possible that God is using your steadfastness amid difficulty to inspire someone else's flagging faith? Yes, you have heard "no" over and over again, but is it possible God is preparing you for a new opportunity you would never have considered if you had already gotten your "yes"?

I'll admit it's hard to see all the possibilities when you're worried about being able to hang on until tomorrow. It takes a very special type of heart to keep believing during the hard times. But it helps to remember that God specializes in the unexpected. He is into the unpredictable, the unlooked-for. He is the original author of the surprise ending.

Joshua: A Longing to Know God

I would like to introduce you to another one of my faith heroes. Joshua was one of Moses' protégés, along with Caleb, one of the few who were able to catch a glimpse of the great leader's vision of God and follow that vision, no matter where it led or how crazy it seemed at the moment.

Joshua had the unique ability to keep believing God was getting ready to do something big. When he was chosen as one of the twelve spies to sneak into the Promised Land and check out the lay of the country, he and Caleb were able to see that God had prepared for His people an abundant homeland, a place "flowing with milk and honey" (Exodus 3:8). However, the other ten spies could see only the problems.

What made the difference? All twelve spies saw the same land, the same people, the same opportunities, and the same risks. Yet Joshua and Caleb came away believing God could deliver the land to His people while the other ten spies were ready to surrender before the battle had even begun.

I believe we get a clue in Exodus 33. This is where the Bible tells about the Tent of Meeting, the place Moses set up outside the main camp of the Israelites, where he would go to meet with God. It was an awe-inspiring place. The Bible says that when Moses went there to inquire of God, "the pillar of cloud would come down and stay at the entrance, while the LORD spoke with Moses. Whenever the people saw the pillar of cloud standing at the entrance to the tent, they all stood and worshiped" (Exodus 33:9–10). The Bible goes on to say, "The LORD would speak to Moses face to face, as one speaks to a friend. Then Moses would return to the camp" (Exodus 33:11).

But here is the part I love, at the very end of verse 11, just after Moses leaves to return to the camp: "But his young aide Joshua son of Nun did not leave the tent." Joshua wanted more than anything to be in God's presence at the Tent of Meeting. He had a longing to know God that was even stronger than his desire to be with Moses, the man he admired so much. I believe that is why he and Caleb saw opportunity where everybody else saw only danger. Joshua spent time with God. He had a deep longing to be as well acquainted as possible with his Creator.

Joshua knew God—knew His character, His nature, and His purposes. That's why he and Caleb had such confidence. Their knowledge of God did not permit them to believe God would bring His people all the way to the Promised Land, only to abandon them. They had an unshakable confidence that God would complete everything He had promised.

Time with God Is Essential

To accomplish anything of consequence in our lives, it is essential that we spend time with God. After all, if we don't know the One who has promised to watch over us, how can we trust in His provision?

Even little babies know this. The first time you are introduced to a baby, you can stand and grin and coo and hold out your hands invitingly as much as you want, but that child is not going to go to you until his or her parent gives assurance, by word or by touch, that it's okay. Why? Because the child knows and trusts the parent implicitly. The parent and the child have spent time together; the child knows the parent will not willingly bring danger into the environment. It has been proven over and over.

This is true of just about any relationship you can think of. The deepest trust comes as a result of the greatest investment of time together. In a marriage, in parenting, in a work relationship, in church leadership, in friendship, on a team, in a musical group—you name it. You learn to trust people by spending lots of time with them, by getting to know them.

In the same way, in order to develop a deep and lasting trust in God, you have to spend time with Him. You have to spend time reading His word and conversing with Him in prayer.

If you want to live a life of confidence and purpose, you have to find ways to stay connected with Jesus, day to day and moment to moment. You need to build into your daily routine times of intimacy with Christ, breathing His spirit deeply into your being.

One of the best ways to do this is to focus on prayer. An effective prayer life is an essential part of building trust with our Heavenly Father. It's something we all desperately need, yet often neglect. In fact, Christians often feel guiltier about their prayer life—or lack of one—than almost any other aspect of their spiritual life.

How about you? Ever feel guilty about how little time you spend in prayer or about not being able to stay focused during your prayer time? Ever wonder if you're praying the right way or worry that you should be doing something different?

John Ortberg talks about this in his book, *The Me I Want to Be*:

> When I pray, I end up praying about things I think I *should* be concerned about: missionaries, world peace, and global warming. But my mind keeps wandering toward stuff I am genuinely concerned about. The way to let my talking flow into praying is this: *I must pray what is in me, not what I wish were in me.*[10]

I think Ortberg is onto an incredible breakthrough. The more I've started to pray what's *in* me instead of what I *wish* were in me, the more I've been able to truly enjoy my time with God and connect with him more frequently.

This really gets into a deeper issue of prayer. I think many of us live with the idea that somehow God doesn't hear or see certain things in our life. We actually think that we can fool God by praying about one thing, even though we're thinking and focused on another.

Sometimes I have to laugh as I watch my three boys fight at dinner over who's going to ask the blessing. It usually starts with my oldest, Jett, saying something like, "I think Gage should pray tonight." Gage will respond, "No, I think Brewer should pray." And then Brewer will pipe in, "No, I prayed last night. It's Jett's turn."

Just a few nights ago I asked my son Gage if he would bless the food. He looked at me with these big puppy-dog eyes and said, "Dad, I want to. I really do. But I'm just way too hungry to pray tonight. Someone else is going to have to do it."

The whole routine is not only funny, but quite ironic, because it apparently never crosses those boys' minds that maybe God can actually hear them arguing about not wanting to pray. But no adult would ever think that way . . . right?

Sure we would. We do it all the time. In fact, this is exactly why people use a different voice when they pray! It's why we think we have to close our eyes or be in a certain position with our hands held just right. It's why we pray about stuff we think sounds spiritual instead of just saying what's truly on our hearts and minds.

You will experience a breakthrough in your prayer life when you discover that you don't have to pray anything other than what's on your mind and in your heart. This is when you begin to discover that every moment and every thought is another opportunity to connect with your Father in heaven. This is when those moments, each and every one of them, become an opportunity to build that much-needed trust with God.

When you make time with God part of your way of

living—when you learn, to use the phrase coined by the great monastic thinker Brother Lawrence, to "practice the presence of God"—you will begin to see that your vision is being continually corrected in its focus. You will begin to realize you are no longer surprised by conflict or adversity because your trust in God has placed Him, rather than your situation, at the center of your life.

 ## Chapter Two in Review

Key Ideas

1. Never forget that you don't know the whole story about other people. Some of the most successful people you can imagine have also dealt with the most devastating failures you can imagine.

2. Only because Joseph was willing to keep on trusting God—despite his circumstances, and despite the lack of all visible evidence of the possibility of a good outcome—was he able to reach the day when he could say to his brothers, "You meant it for harm, but God meant it for good."

3. We are most often focused on what is happening *to* us, but God is more concerned about what is happening *in* us.

4. Joshua knew God—knew His character, His nature, and His purposes. That's why he and Caleb had such confidence. Their knowledge of God did not permit

them to believe God would bring His people all the way to the Promised Land, only to abandon them. They had an unshakable confidence that God would complete everything He had promised to do.

5. The deepest trust comes as a result of the greatest investment of time together.

Reflection Questions

1. Why do you think we are willing to accept that we must do resistance training to strengthen our muscles but less willing to accept that our spiritual "muscles" need resistance training, too?

2. Have you ever looked at someone who seemed to be experiencing a perfect life or an easy time, only to discover later that the person was going through deep struggles? What effect did learning of their struggles have on you?

3. If you were making a movie about Joseph's life, what would you title it?

4. Think of a friendship that you have lost because of spending little time together—either because of distance, changes in life direction, or other reasons. How long did it take before you began to realize the relationship was fading?

5. Have you ever had a dream that you believed contained a real-life message? What made you think this? What, if anything, did you do about it?

Your Next Step

Talk to someone who, you believe, is "living the dream." Ask that person to tell you about the toughest obstacle he or she has faced so far.

THREE

HANG ON TO WHAT LASTS

"Time is filled with swift transition,
Naught of earth unmoved can stand.
Build your hopes on things eternal,
Hold to God's unchanging hand."
—Jennie Wilson (American hymn)

Everybody knows the story of the Three Little Pigs. There is much to admire in these enterprising porkers: they were hard workers, they relied on each other, and they knew better than to talk to strangers. But two of the pigs had a problem. They didn't know how to build something that would last. The first pig's house of straw and, later, the second pig's house of sticks both succumbed to the attacks of the Big Bad Wolf. Only when they sheltered in their brother's house of bricks did they find safety from their adversary.

Many of us have a similar problem with our perception of what will last. We build our dreams with the materials we have at hand, thinking that what we build will keep us safe. But all too often, we are building with straw or sticks, and our efforts are vulnerable to the ravages of circumstance.

The fact is that if our ideas, inspiration, and hopes depend on anything other than God, we are building with the wrong materials. Placing our reliance on money, on our careers, or even on the people we love will, at some time or other, subject us to despair.

Now, please understand: God knows we need money in order to live. God expects us to work to the best of our ability at the tasks and opportunities He sends our way. And God places people in our lives to love and support us and also for us to love and support. None of these things are bad in themselves, but they become a problem when we place our ultimate dependence on them. The only ultimate security any of us has is our relationship with God. When we try to get that from something else—even a good thing—we are going to get ourselves into trouble.

The good news is that God wants to be in relationship with us. As a matter of fact, He is always making Himself available to us, if only we are willing to respond. It is His nature to be in communion with His creation and especially with humankind, since we are made in His image. We can see the evidence of this in God's earliest dealings with people, as shown all the way back in the beginning of the Bible, in Genesis.

Walking in the Garden

There is a phrase in the story of Adam and Eve in the Garden of Eden that is very telling. In Genesis 3, we have the heart-breaking story of the temptation and fall of Adam and Eve when they succumbed to the deceit of the devil and disobeyed God. But tucked into that story is a little phrase I find fascinating. After Adam and Eve sinned, the Bible says they heard "the sound of the Lord God as he was walking in the garden in the cool of the day" (Genesis 3:8). I just love to think about that! God, the Creator of the universe, apparently liked to come and take a stroll in the garden He had created, once the heat of the day was past.

I can easily imagine, in the days before Adam and Eve's disobedience, that the three of them walked in the garden together. After all, there was no flaw in the relationship at that earlier time. Why would God not choose to enjoy the company of the beings into whom He had breathed "the breath of life" (Genesis 2:7) as He walked along in the cool of the evening?

It seems reasonable to assume that, just as God enjoyed seeing what He had made (He pronounced it all "very good"), He also enjoyed the company of the man and woman to whom He had entrusted care of His creation. In my mind's eye, I can imagine the three of them, hand in hand, walking and talking as God explains to Adam and Eve all the beauty He has fashioned for their enjoyment and contentment.

Of course, as we now know, that delightful companionship

with God would come to a tragic end. Through Satan's guile, the perfect, innocent relationship Adam and Eve enjoyed with God would be broken by sin (Genesis 3:13–24). No more would humankind enjoy the blessing of conversing with God while walking side by side through the beauty of a sinless world.

But despite humanity's sin—from the fall of Adam and Eve until the very present—God has never stopped loving us. He has never stopped longing to be with us, to take our hands and walk with us through the garden. Our God *wants to be with us.* In fact, He will stop at nothing to heal and restore the relationship that was broken by sin so long ago.

This desire of God for intimacy and companionship with you is what makes possible the trust we see in people like Joseph, Joshua, or the deeply spiritual people of our own day. You don't have to wait until you are "ready" or "spiritually mature" or "qualified" in order to walk with God. He will come to you! But He will not force Himself upon you. It is an amazing and frightening thought to realize that the all-powerful Creator of the universe has made one thing out-of-bounds, even for Himself: He will not compel us to love or obey Him. He wants us to choose Him freely.

So, the question is not whether God wants to be with you. Instead, the question is, do *you* want to be with Him?

Taking a Walk with God

Think for a second about all that is implied by taking a walk with someone. First and most obvious, we don't take a walk with a concept or a theory. We take a walk with a person! The very act implies some sort of relationship. (I realize many of us also take walks with our dogs, but, really, don't we do that for many of the same reasons? Part of the reason we walk dogs is for companionship, right?)

When was the last time somebody at your office called a meeting and said, "Okay, let's all discuss these five action points as we walk down the street"? I'm guessing never. We walk with people when we want relationship. Our primary purpose is not to do business or to make decisions but rather to explore or deepen our connection to the other person.

When I think about taking a walk with someone, I think about the walks I've enjoyed with my wife. I also think about the times, walking with my kids, when one of them has spontaneously reached out and grabbed my hand as we went along. I'm telling you, there aren't many moments better than that! And the motivating factor behind these walks wasn't the exercise or the activity; it was the opportunity to spend time together, to get to know one another a little better.

That's what God wants to do with you. He wants to spend time with you, so your relationship can become deeper and richer. God isn't a concept or a theory. He is a person who has desires and purposes—and one of His desires is to be with you!

Take a moment to soak in that thought.

As a matter of fact, there is nothing you can do that will make God *not* want to be with you. There is nothing you can do to cause Him to give up on you. There is only your choice: Do you want to be with God or not? He is holding out His hand to you at this very moment, asking, "Want to take a walk?"

How will you answer?

Unquenchable Love

I remember one night when I was praying over my younger son, who was asleep on his bed. As I prayed for him, the thought suddenly entered my mind that this precious little boy, whose heart is so pure, would one day grow up and become a man. At the time, this little guy was pretty much incapable of doing anything we would consider to be a major wrong, but I knew it wouldn't always be that way.

It is a fundamental fact that, in this life, you reap what you sow. That is just as true for innocent little six-year-old boys and girls as it is for grown men and women. All the way through life, the decisions we make determine the course of our lives.

Sometimes we think we can avoid the law of consequences, but we can't. Our decisions and actions will always come home to roost, for good or ill. And as I prayed for my son, the reality and implications of this for his life suddenly became very real to me.

In his life, he will have to make many choices—and it is possible that some of his choices will not please me. In fact, it is possible—probably likely—that he could make choices that will be personally devastating to me. It is also possible that some of his decisions could have life-changing consequences for him—both good and bad. And yet, I will still be his father, and he will still be my son. No matter what he does for the rest of his life—whether he makes good decisions or not—there is no changing that. He will always be my boy.

If I can feel that unalterable commitment to my son, just imagine what God feels for you! What kind of difference would it make in your life if you knew absolutely that no matter what you do or how badly you mess up, God is always going to be there, wanting more than anything to take you back into His love?

I think a lot of folks are paralyzed by a false picture of God. They have the image of a stern old man who is just waiting for them to screw up so He can chew them out and tell them everything they've done wrong. Once again, I think about my own children. When they mess up, most of the time they know it. They are usually very well aware that what they have done or said is not pleasing to their mom or to me. In that situation, their instinct is to avoid us.

You probably remember the same thing in your own life. When you stayed out past your curfew, did you walk into the house and march into your parents' bedroom to be sure they knew you came in late? No, you avoided that conversation as long as you could! Or when roughhousing in the living room led to a broken crystal vase, were you eager for your mom to get home so she could see her shattered finery? Probably not.

But just as surely as your parents still loved you when you stayed out late or broke their stuff, God still loves you when you mess up. Don't avoid Him! He already knows what you've done—heck, He knew the second you even started to think about doing whatever it was you did. You can't hide from God—and there's no need to! More than anything else, He wants you to come back to Him, say you're sorry, and let Him help you do better next time.

Don't avoid the conversation with God. Take a walk with Him. He's always ready to spend time with you.

The God with Open Arms

Some of us have a difficult time accepting the reality that God actually does want to be with us. Often, because of traumatic experiences in our childhoods or our more recent pasts, we have a hard time imagining that anyone—God included—could possibly value us. We ask ourselves, *Why should God want to be with me? Just look at how messed up I am.* Or we may think, *I haven't been able to rely on anyone in my life. At one time or another, they've all let me down. Why would God be any different?*

The sad truth is that, when we say these types of things to ourselves, we're right. We *are* messed up. And at one time or another, every human relationship we've ever had *has* let us down.

I love my wife more than I love any other human being currently on the planet. I am committed to her welfare with every fiber of my being. She is part of me, and I can't imagine my life without her. But despite all that, she has let me down. And guess what? I've done the same to her. At times I've brought her great joy, but I've also been the one to bring her great pain.

I love my boys. I would lie down in front of a moving train to keep them safe. I have no greater joy than to see them doing well, but they don't always do what I want them to. Sometimes, they even do and say things that hurt me. And, as hard as I try to avoid it, sometimes I'm not a perfect dad. I don't always act in their best interest.

The fact is, every relationship you have with a human being, no matter how committed and well-intentioned, is flawed. Sometimes you let them down; sometimes they let you down. And what that means is that, over time, we learn to hold back in our relationships, out of self-defense. We know that, at some point, we're going to hurt or be hurt, so we try to protect ourselves by keeping a little something in reserve, by not committing 100 percent at every moment. And then we project that same behavior onto our relationship with God.

Our human experience makes it exceedingly difficult to believe that God is 100 percent faithful, that He will never let us down. We cannot ever wrap our minds completely around His unconditional, everlasting, indestructible love for us. God is forever standing with open arms, waiting to receive us, but we find it hard to fully embrace Him. And yet that is exactly what we must do.

Let Go and Grab Hold

The simple fact is that in order to learn to embrace uncertainty and move forward despite your fears, you've got to turn loose of your uncertainty. As long as you're holding on tight to your misgivings about God, you can't grab on to His faithfulness.

I've got a friend who is a rock climber. He tells me that as long as you're just hanging on where you are, it's impossible to go any higher. I've never done any rock climbing, but I can imagine that when you're fifty, seventy-five, or a hundred feet up on a steep rock face, having both hands and both feet dug into a good, tight hold would feel pretty good. When gravity is working against you, it's nice to know you can hang on to something.

But guess what? Hanging on where you are guarantees that you won't go anywhere—up or down. To make progress in either direction, you've got to release your present security and reach out.

I believe that many of us, in our battles with our fears and troubles, have given up on progress and settled for just not falling. I understand that impulse. I really do. But I believe we have a God who longs to reach out and take us by the hand and draw us up toward higher ground. And as long as our fists are clenched around the things we presently trust, we can't grip God's outstretched hand. We won't go any higher.

Listen to me: no matter what you are holding on to right now—whether it is your 401(k), your job title, your protective mistrust of the people around you, your anger at a friend's betrayal, your dependence upon another person, or whatever it is you think makes you feel safe—you will be more secure once you've let go of that and grabbed God's hand. The faithfulness of God is stronger than whatever fears or challenges are holding you back.

Nothing except God lasts forever. Everything else will fade. And one day, that thing, person, or situation you're grasping so tightly will turn to dust in your hand.

Only God lasts. Grab His hand. He promises He will never leave nor forsake you (Deuteronomy 31:6).

 Chapter Three in Review

Key Ideas

1. The fact is that if our dreams depend on anything other than God, we are building with the wrong materials.
2. God has never stopped loving us. He has never stopped longing to be with us, to take our hands and walk with us through the garden. Our God *wants to be with us*. In fact, He will stop at nothing to heal and restore the relationship that was broken by sin so long ago.
3. What kind of difference would it make in your life if you knew absolutely that no matter what you do or how badly you mess up, God is always going to be there, wanting more than anything to take you back into His love?
4. As long as you're holding on tight to your misgivings about God, you can't grab on to His faithfulness.

Reflection Questions

1. List the things or qualities you see many people substituting for God as the foundation of their lives.

What makes it easier for us to trust in these things than to trust in God?

2. What is the difference between securing what we need to live (money, human relationships, career, etc.) and placing our primary trust in these things? How can we avoid crossing that line?

3. What is your greatest obstacle to believing God really does want to spend time with you?

4. What sin do you think is the worst sin? Do you believe God is big enough to forgive that sin?

Your Next Step

Sometime when you are alone, place two chairs facing each other. Seat yourself in one, and imagine Jesus seated in the other. Talk out loud to Jesus just as you would to an understanding friend. Say everything that is on your heart. As you speak to Jesus, believe that He is listening to you and looking into your eyes. (This also works when you are driving alone; you can let Jesus ride shotgun—just don't let him take the wheel.)

FOUR

EMBRACE UNCERTAINTY

*"If a man will begin with certainties, he shall
end in doubts; but if he will be content to begin
with doubts, he shall end in certainties."*
—Francis Bacon

There's an old story about two farmers shooting the breeze down at the feed store on a Saturday morning.

One says to the other, "You got your cotton all planted?"

"Nope," says the other. "Decided not to plant any cotton this year; I'm too worried about the boll weevils."

"Well, then I guess you're putting all your land in corn?"

"Nope. Might not rain. Corn's got to have rain."

By now, the first farmer is scratching his head. "So, you aren't making a cotton crop, and you aren't planting corn. I guess you're relying on your winter wheat to carry you through?"

The second farmer shook his head. "Didn't put in any wheat. Too scared of the armyworms."

The first farmer is openly amazed. "No wheat, no corn, no cotton . . . so, you aren't making any kind of a crop this year at all?"

"That's right. This year, I decided to just play it safe."

Play It Safe? Or Trust God?

Of course, we all recognize the folly of "playing it safe" by doing nothing at all. And yet, so often, by holding on to whatever we associate with security, we guarantee that we live paralyzed lives: not the life that God intends for us.

The Bible says, in Ecclesiastes 11:4, "Whoever watches the wind will not plant; whoever looks at the clouds will not reap." It's a very true principle. Like the overly cautious farmer in the story above, if we wait until we have absolute certainty to do something, it won't ever get done.

In order to combat the fears that keep you up at night, you must embrace uncertainty. Remember how the story of Joseph teaches us that complete clarity only comes with hindsight? Most of the time, you will not be able to see the end from the beginning. You must take the first step, then the next, believing that, as you move forward, the rest of the path will be revealed.

In this connection, we have to remember that when we move forward in faith, we are not simply rolling the dice. Our attitude should not be, *Well, there's no such thing as a sure thing, so I might as well try and see what happens.* Instead, when we release our own attempts at security and grasp God's hand, our thinking should be, *I know that the future will always be uncertain, but I also know that God is faithful, no matter what the future holds.* Never forget that you are not trusting to blind chance; you are trusting the God who longs to be with you.

Trust, in fact, is the foundation of any relationship. In marriage, in business, in parenting, trust is the keystone on which everything else rests. And yet, trust in God does not come naturally or easily. It must be learned, and then it must be exercised frequently. Like a muscle that grows with use, trust in God increases the more we employ it. But also like a muscle, it will atrophy with disuse. I love the way Brennan Manning explains it in his book, *Ruthless Trust*:

> I cannot simply will myself to trust. What outrageous irony: the one thing that I am responsible for throughout my life I cannot generate. . . . But such is the meaning of radical dependence. . . . What does lie within my power is paying attention to the faithfulness of Jesus. That's what I am asked to do: pay attention to Jesus throughout my journey, remembering his kindnesses.[1]

When we embrace uncertainty and grasp God's hand, He will give us opportunity after opportunity to exercise our "trust muscles." Like a mother bird who knows that, at some point, the fledglings must be forced out of the nest in order to learn to fly, God lovingly permits us to learn how to pay attention to the faithfulness of Jesus in various circumstances to gain experience of dependence on Him.

I don't know how many of you share my attitude toward using GPS apps, but I get really impatient when I'm trying to follow them. All the GPS will do is give me the next turn I need to make, but that's not good enough for me. I want to look two or three turns ahead, but the GPS map isn't going to work that way. I want to see the whole route, laid out for my approval or disapproval, but what I get is the next turn I need to make, the distance to the next checkpoint. And so, what I have to learn to do is trust the app to tell me as much as I need to know in order to get that much closer to my destination.

Fortunately, God is a lot more trustworthy than any GPS app! (Anyone who has found him- or herself either going around in circles or driving miles out of the way while trying to follow Siri's directions knows what I mean.) But just like taking a trip with GPS, our journey of faith is, most of the time, a one-step-at-a-time process.

While I know what step I'm on right now, I don't know what steps or what turns may be lying ahead tomorrow or in the next days and weeks. And that brings about some fear and anxiety for me. I bet some of you feel paralyzed right now because you're not sure what steps await you. You've got big questions.

When am I going to get married?

When is the marriage going to get better?

Will I ever find a job that I love?

Will I ever find freedom from this addictive cycle of sin?

You'd do anything to be able to see into the future and see steps six through nine. But right now, maybe you're on step five. Can you stay there and patiently wait and trust for step six, even without seeing all the way to the end?

Once again, this means that we must embrace uncertainty as a part of our exercise in trusting God. A few years ago, Stormie Omartian wrote a book entitled *Just Enough Light for the Step I'm On*. I love that! It captures perfectly the nature of our journey toward trust in God. He will always show us the next step He wants us to take. He will not usually lay out the entire route for our inspection.

What Trust Is . . . and What It Isn't

Webster defines *trust* as "dependence on someone or something." But particularly in our American culture, we have a difficult time with the notion of "dependence." To us, the word carries a connotation of weakness, of not being able to take care of ourselves. The images and icons our culture admires most are not usually characterized by the word "dependent," are they? Captain America, Rosie the Riveter, the Marlboro Man, and Katniss Everdeen in *Hunger Games* are all characters who exude strength, resourcefulness, and independence.

Men, especially, can have a deep reluctance to appear "dependent." Most often, our society expects a man to be the strong supporter, the fighter, the rock, and the protector. He is not supposed to be dependent.

But I think some reframing is called for here. What if we were to think of depending on God not as the absence of strength but, rather, as the presence of courage? Because, after all, you need courage in order to release what has provided your security and grasp the hand of an unseen God. It takes courage to admit that your own resources are inadequate and to follow God, one step at a time, when the end is not apparent. Courage is required to move forward in the face of uncertainty.

It comes down to this: there are two mutually exclusive worldviews at work. In one, each of us must be in control of our own destiny. We are the ultimate masters of our fate, and we must depend on ourselves and our own resources in order to succeed in life.

In the other worldview, God is in control. While we may and should do the best we can with the talents and opportunities we have, ultimately we realize that God is the only one we can truly depend on. Through the strength and provision God provides, we succeed.

It all goes back to the idea of "lifting my eyes" to focus on the true source of my help and strength. If I believe the Creator of heaven and earth is watching over me with vigilant care, then my trust is based on so much more than anything I can provide through my own resources. If I am focused on God's power and provision, then I am operating on the only truly reliable foundation in the universe.

Don't make the mistake of thinking that trust is primarily a state of mind or some sort of ability to "think positive." In fact, some of the people who trust God most deeply and absolutely are also those who have experienced great pain. Once again, Brennan Manning's *Ruthless Trust* puts the matter in perspective:

> In explaining the growth of his faith, psychiatrist Gerald May writes, "I know that God is loving and that God's loving is trustworthy. I know this directly, through the experience of my life. There have been plenty of times of doubt, especially when I used to believe that trusting God's goodness meant I would not be hurt. But having been hurt quite a bit, I know God's goodness goes deeper than all pleasure and pain; it embraces them both."[2]

As these words show so clearly, the kind of trust in God I am talking about does not pale even in the face of difficulty, pain, or heartbreak. It perseveres, believing that if heartbreak comes into our lives, God will provide enough strength to hang on and enough sustenance to meet the challenge.

Trust is also not some sort of blind leap into the unknown. In fact, in many ways it is the opposite. It ultimately depends on the type of knowledge that only comes with long acquaintance and intimate understanding. When I know the character of God and how He has acted in my life in the past, my trust in Him becomes more a matter of clear-eyed reliance than blind dependence. When I trust in God, I am acting on the conviction that He knows more about real life than I do.

But in our society, one of the steepest obstacles to trust is the overriding cynicism of our age. For much of the past three centuries or so, Western society has come more and more to believe that the skeptic is inherently smarter than the person who believes. Thus, trusting in God is often seen as simple-minded at best and superstitious at worst. But cynicism can corrode the soul. It is dangerous because it proceeds out of pride: the need to "not be taken in," to prove oneself wiser and more perceptive than the "foolish masses."

In *The Last Battle*, the last of C. S. Lewis's books set in the land of Narnia, there is a scene that is both beautiful and haunting. It occurs when Aslan, the great lion who symbolizes Christ, has defeated all his enemies and is about to welcome those who love him into the unfading land that will last forever. Some dwarves who opposed Aslan are huddled off to the side. They are utterly convinced that they alone see things as they really are. To these unbelieving dwarves, Aslan is a fake. Not only that, but they are convinced they are imprisoned inside a stinking, dark shed, when they are actually sitting in the middle of a beautiful, sunlit meadow. When Aslan tries to give these dwarves delicious food to eat, they insist that it is garbage. When he offers them rich wine, they say it is water from an animal's trough. To the very end, though, they congratulate themselves on not falling for any of Aslan's "trickery."

This is what cynicism can do to the human spirit. It can blind us to the rich blessings surrounding us. In our "wisdom," we are convinced that the gifts offered by our loving God are fakes, superstitions, and not to be trusted. The cynic cannot trust in the wisdom of God, for he believes himself to be the only source of wisdom in the universe.

Another obstacle to embracing uncertainty is our own natural need to be in control. If we place our reliance in God, then we are no longer the captains of our own ships, and for some of us, that is a thought we can't handle.

I don't know if there's a place in Scripture that we see this more clearly than when the Israelites had been delivered from four hundred years of captivity and God brings them to the edge of the Promised Land. This was the life that He so desperately wanted His people to live, but it was going to require them facing a few fears along the way.

So their leader, Moses, sent out twelve spies to check out the land to see what it's like.

> They came back to Moses and Aaron and the whole Israelite community at Kadesh in the Desert of Paran. There they reported to them and to the whole assembly and showed them the fruit of the land. They gave Moses this account: "We went into the land to which you sent us, and it does flow with milk and honey! Here is its fruit. But the people who live there are powerful, and the cities are fortified and very large. We even saw descendants of Anak there. The Amalekites live in the Negev; the Hittites, Jebusites and Amorites live in the hill country; and the Canaanites live near the sea and along the Jordan." (Numbers 13:26–29)

Isn't it interesting how they couldn't help but notice the beauty of the land? They couldn't help but think, *This must be the place for us.* But their hopes and dreams quickly fizzled as they got focused on, *But* . . .

It's beautiful . . . *but* there are people already there and they're huge.

It's got to be the land for us . . . *but* we could never take those guys on. They'll crush us.

But in the sea of fear rose a courageous voice. I have no real formulas for success, but what I do know is this: if you try to please everyone you will fail. There are times in this journey we're all on that you must have the courage to act against an expert's advice. That's what we see in the next verse: "Then Caleb silenced the people before Moses and said, 'We should go up and take possession of the land, for we can certainly do it'" (Numbers 13:30).

Even though everyone else had panicked and wanted to turn back, Joshua and one other spy named Caleb said they thought it could be done—with God's help.

Sadly, fear won out that day. We will never know for sure what might have happened had the people not allowed their fear to overwhelm them. That day, the Israelites proved to all of us that it's possible to be delivered to freedom—but to not actually be free.

What Trust Looks Like

The trust that allows us to embrace uncertainty has three aspects: belief in the provision of God, belief in the promises of God, and belief in the power of God. And one of the stories from the Bible that best illustrates this type of trust is the story of Daniel.

Daniel had been taken from the land of Judah as a young boy. Along with many of his friends, he was marched off to the city of Babylon when Nebuchadnezzar, the king of Babylon, conquered Jerusalem. As was the custom at the time, Nebuchadnezzar had the best and brightest of Judah's youths brought to his royal palace, so they could be trained in the ways of the Babylonian court. They would go on to become officers, counselors, and aides in Nebuchadnezzar's government. And also, by robbing Judah of the cream of the crop, he was depriving the conquered land of those who would, in the future, be most able to form and lead a resistance movement.

Daniel proved to be one of the best of the best. He quickly advanced in the service of Nebuchadnezzar, but because of his deep faith, he was able to do this without forgetting the God of his people. In fact, much like Joseph in Pharaoh's court, Daniel was able to interpret the dreams that troubled Nebuchadnezzar. As a result, he became a trusted advisor, not only to Nebuchadnezzar, but also to the Persian king, Darius, who would conquer Babylon years later. Such was Daniel's wisdom that, even in the midst of a violent regime change, he was still valued and protected.

As Daniel became an old man, he continued his habit of going into his room, kneeling down in the direction of Jerusalem, and praying to God. He did this three times a day, even as he was faithfully serving King Darius.

Darius let it be known that he was considering having all his other satraps and advisors report to Daniel. Needless to say, in a royal court, jealousy can run rampant, and the other advisors and officials didn't like the prospect of Daniel's promotion one bit. So, they hit upon a scheme to get Daniel out of the way. They convinced the king to proclaim a law forbidding anyone to pray to any God other than King Darius himself. Actually, such a loyalty oath was not uncommon among other Middle Eastern societies of that time, and it probably sounded like a reasonable plan to Darius—not to mention it stroked his ego. So, he had the law drawn up, and he signed it. Oh, and the punishment for violating the law? Offenders would be tossed into a lions' den.

Of course, Daniel knew what the law meant, and he also was perceptive enough to understand the intent of those who had influenced the king to proclaim it. So what did he do? He did exactly the same thing he had been doing every day of his life. He went to his room, kneeled down in the direction of Jerusalem, and prayed to God.

Now, I'd like to pause here and point out something interesting. The only thing we know about Daniel's prayer is that it involved "giving thanks to his God, just as he had done before" (Daniel 6:10). Scripture does not suggest that he prayed for deliverance from the scheming of the other officials, nor does it hint that he prayed for Darius to see what Daniel's enemies were up to. All we know is that Daniel gave thanks to God and that he was apparently in the long habit of doing this.

This goes back to an idea we talked about earlier: everyday

courage. Daniel knew the other officials had it in for him, and he knew that if he kept on praying to God, they would catch him. And that is exactly what happened. But none of this prevented Daniel from doing the next right thing. Because he trusted God more than he feared the other officials or the king's new law, he kept right on with his daily routine of offering thanksgiving to God. He embraced uncertainty.

King Darius realized too late that he had been played. When Daniel's accusers told the king Daniel had violated the new law, the king was "greatly distressed" (Daniel 6:14), and spends the whole day trying to find a loophole in the law to get Daniel out of trouble. But, in the end, he cannot; and as the sentence is being carried out, Darius exclaimed to Daniel, "May your God, whom you serve continually, rescue you!" (v. 16).

That phrase, "whom you serve continually," is telling. It indicates that Daniel was known to Darius as someone who was always pursuing the service of God. For Daniel, walking with God wasn't an emergency plan; it was a way of life.

Most of us know how the story turns out. Daniel is indeed tossed in the lions' den, but God sent an angel to prevent the lions from harming him. King Darius, distraught at the idea of losing his most trusted advisor, can't sleep or eat. The next morning, he got up at the crack of dawn and rushed down to the place the lions were kept. He called out, "Daniel, servant of the living God, has your God, whom you serve continually, been able to rescue you from the lions?" (Daniel 6:20).

Daniel told the king that he was fine and how God sent an angel to shut the mouths of the lions. He added that he had never done any wrong to Darius. Darius ordered that Daniel be taken out of the lions' den, and the Bible says "no wound was found on him, because he had trusted in his God" (Daniel 6:23).

Matters didn't turn out so well for Daniel's accusers, however. Darius had them tossed into the lions' den—along with their entire families! And God provided no protective angel for them.

Finally, Darius had a new law proclaimed throughout the Persian Empire:

> I issue a decree that in every part of my kingdom people must
> fear and reverence the God of Daniel.
>> For he is the living God and he endures forever; . . .
>> He rescues and he saves; he performs signs and wonders . . .
>> He has rescued Daniel from the power of the lions.
> (Daniel 6:26–27)

Now, here is a statistic that I find very interesting: the book of Daniel contains 153 verses detailing what Daniel's life was like during all the time leading up to the lion's den. But there is only one verse that gives any information about what his life was like inside the lion's den, and that verse is second-hand information, as reported to Darius by Daniel. In other words, the experience in the lions' den is not the main point of the story of Daniel, even though we most often think of him as "Daniel in the lions' den." No, the heartbeat of the story is that, every day of his life, Daniel exercised ordinary, day-to-day courage. And that is what enabled him to do the next right thing—to embrace uncertainty because of his carefully formed habit of trusting God.

Daniel believed in the provision of God—that God would be able to take care of him, no matter what. He believed in the promise of God—that the Creator of heaven and earth would watch over him and would not let his foot slip. He believed in the power of God—that God was able to protect him, even in a den full of hungry lions.

Putting First Things First

As I read the story of Daniel, I am reminded in a powerful way that, in order to get to the answer, you must first live the life that leads to the answer. I have observed that the people who are getting up every single day and walking hand-in-hand with God are not the people who spend a lot of time asking the question, "What is God's purpose for my life?" No, they are too busy trusting God and doing the next right thing to spend time worrying about whether they are doing what God wants them to do.

But too many of us are like me with the GPS map. We want to see the last step before we take the first step. We spend so much time trying to see the end that we never get around to the beginning.

I love the scene in *Indiana Jones and the Last Crusade* when it dawns on Jones that the only way to reach the chamber where the Holy Grail is kept is to step out into what appears to be the empty space above a chasm. "It's a leap of faith," he says to himself, just before stepping off what looks like a sheer cliff. But the path materializes beneath his feet. He has to take the step in order to find the path.

In the same way, the life of faith requires taking the next step, even when you may not be sure where the path is leading. You can be sure of one thing, though: the Maker of heaven and earth will not let your foot slip; He who watches over you will not slumber.

 Chapter Four in Review

Key Ideas

1. Most of the time, you will not be able to see the end from the beginning. You must take the first step, then the next, believing that, as you move forward, the rest of the path will be revealed.

2. Trust in God does not come naturally or easily. It must be learned, and then it must be exercised frequently. Like a muscle that grows with use, trust in God increases the more we employ it.

3. What if we were to think of depending on God not as the absence of strength but, rather, as the presence of courage?

4. Trust has three aspects: belief in the provision of God, belief in the promises of God, and belief in the power of God.

5. In order to get to the answer, you must first live the life that leads to the answer.

Reflection Questions

1. Are you facing a decision or situation in your life that requires a leap of faith? What is preventing you from taking that first step of trust in God?
2. What obstacles most often keep us from doing the next right thing?
3. What is the difference between embracing uncertainty by trusting God and merely employing a positive attitude?

Your Next Step

For a week, try to think of three new things each day that you are thankful to God for. As you pray and thank God for His provision in these matters, ask Him to give you greater confidence in an area or circumstance where you are feeling anxious or worried.

FIVE

LEARN TO WAIT

"When in doubt, do nothing, but continue to wait on God. When action is needed, light will come."
—J. I. Packer

In 1989, Chuck Snyder wrote a book titled *I Prayed for Patience and Other Horror Stories.* Everyone I've ever known who saw the cover of that book reacted with a smile, a laugh, or a knowing nod. We've all been there. We've all prayed that famous prayer, "Lord, give me patience—*right now!*" But of course, what we come to realize is that, frequently, a prayer for patience is accompanied by opportunities to practice it.

Often we desire God's power, but we aren't willing to accept God's calendar. But God is bound by neither our particular priorities nor our schedule. And really, if God is who we believe Him to be, it couldn't be any other way, could it?

This reminds me of the plaque often seen in office cubicles: "A lack of planning on your part does not automatically create an emergency on my part." Too much of the time, we want God to react to our "emergencies." Because we are at the center of our own universe, and because our difficulties are therefore the most important matter in existence, we have trouble understanding why God can't see the urgency in the situation that we see.

In the Waiting Room

We've all spent time in life's waiting room, haven't we? Sometimes, we're waiting on a child to see the folly of the decisions he has made, and as we wait, the burning questions on our hearts are, *Why won't he change? God, why can't you reach him?*

Or perhaps we're waiting on the outcome of a diagnosis or a treatment. As we wait, our emotions turning each hour into an eternity, we cry out to God, over and over again, "Why can't You heal? If You are good and if You are all-powerful, why do I have to sit in this frightening, lonely waiting room?"

Now, let's take a moment to be honest with each other. When you are sitting at home or with good friends, when the faces are all happy and the kids are all content, when the food is good and the conversation is lively and interesting, is that the moment, for most of us, when we are most aware of our need for God? Is that when we are most prone to admit how much we need Him? Somehow, I doubt it. Usually, it is when we are stuck in one of life's waiting rooms that we realize how utterly helpless and dependent we really are. So, one thing I believe we have to admit about waiting room time is it is where we can most count on remembering our deep need for God's provision.

That's not all bad, by the way. Sometimes, it is when we are at our lowest and weakest that we realize how high and powerful our God is. Paul certainly realized this. In 2 Corinthians 12, he related his struggle with a "thorn in the flesh"—the particular, intimate vulnerability that vexed him most deeply. He tells how he begged God three times to take away this "messenger of Satan." But God answered, "My grace is sufficient for you, for my power is made perfect in weakness" (2 Corinthians 12:9).

Paul goes on to say that he will boast about his weaknesses in order to magnify the power of Christ. In fact, this principle— that God is at His strongest in our lives when we are at our weakest—runs all the way through the Bible. Time after time, when God's people are at their lowest—at the end of hope, with no visible resources to overcome the enemy or the problem at hand—that is precisely the moment God steps in with the most magnificent acts of deliverance.

But we don't get to see God at His most powerful unless we spend some time in the waiting room. When we are highly aware of our own inadequacy, that's when we need to be most aware of God's unlimited ability. When we face the unpleasant and fear-inducing facts of our lives, we must face them with faith in the God who is watching over our lives. When we have nothing else of our own to bring to the struggle, that is when we must rely completely on the victory God has promised.

Why We Can't Wait

One of our biggest problems with waiting is that nothing in our culture teaches us how to do it. In fact, we live in a culture and a society that has done everything possible to eliminate the need for waiting!

Think about it. Let's say it's twenty years ago, and you are an art historian, working on an important publication. If I told you that you could get access to images from the collection of the Louvre Museum in Paris from the comfort of your own home and all you had to do was make a phone call and get on a waiting list, you would jump at the chance. To be able to view iconic works of art without even having to book plane tickets or make hotel reservations? Heck, yeah! Sign me up! The wait would be totally worth it.

But fast-forward to now, and think about what you would do if you Googled the Louvre website and, for whatever reason, it didn't start materializing on your computer screen within about twenty seconds. You'd grimace, shake your head, grumble under your breath about the crummy Internet service provider, and try to find a way to get the site to load quicker. Or you'd move on to something else.

Technology, which promised to place more time at our disposal, has actually just made us more impatient. If the "buy" button on Amazon.com fails to work on the first click, or if the customer service representative leaves me on hold a minute extra, or if the line at Starbucks is too long, it starts to ruin my day.

And what about the way we buy things now? There was a time when people saved up for months to take a trip, to buy a new gadget, or to enjoy a long-anticipated vacation. But now, most often, we use credit to immediately have what we used to have to wait and plan for to get.

We, as a society, are not good at waiting. And it seems to me that with every passing year, we're getting worse. We're becoming "quickaholics" who expect instant results, instant improvement, instant gratification.

In fact, the more important you are and the more resources you have, the less waiting is expected of you. You fly first-class so you can board before everybody else. You're a member of the hotel's Preferred Customer Collective so you can check in online or on the phone.

Similarly, we think that the more spiritually mature we are, the more certainty we have about everything. Somehow, we have the idea that spiritual giants walk around in a serene bubble of certainty, in constant, peaceful contemplation of the victory at the end of the story. They don't have to worry about waiting because their faith takes away all the pain, anxiety, and uncertainty.

But I think it's often just the opposite: God's most deeply committed servants are frequently the ones who live in the most uncertain circumstances. Do you really think that the apostle Paul wasn't anxious to be rescued from the raging storm that was threatening each moment to sink the ship he was on? Do you think that Jesus Christ Himself wasn't daunted by the prospect of the suffering of the cross and the uncertainties of undergoing death? (How many people do you know who have been in such an emotionally extreme place that they actually sweated blood? Jesus did!)

In fact, the way it really works is this: the more spiritually mature you are, the less certainty you require. And the less certainty you require, the more you are able to wait—even under extreme circumstances.

As a pastor I've spent many a long night in the hospital waiting room with families. The waiting room can be a scary place. You'll never feel more utterly out of control than sitting there waiting to hear how a loved one is doing after an accident or following a surgery. There's nothing you can do. *Nothing*— except just sit and wait.

I know it's scary for some of you right now. Fear has gripped you because you feel like all you can do is wait . . . and wait . . . and then wait some more. But you can also know this: the closer you walk with God, the more content you are to simply keep your hand in His and allow Him to take you step-by-step along the path.

The Spiritual Benefits of Waiting

God often uses waiting as a crucible in which to refine our character. Perhaps the prophet Isaiah realized this when he wrote,

"They that wait upon the Lord shall renew their strength; they shall mount up with wings as eagles; they shall run, and not be weary; and they shall walk, and not faint" (Isaiah 40:31 KJV). Faithful waiting on God makes us stronger, not weaker.

Waiting is also a sign of humility. Remember that, long ago, persons of lesser rank who served nobility and royalty were said to "wait upon" them. In a similar way, they were said to "attend" their lords and rulers. Even today, the French word for "wait" is "attend." Maybe there is something to learn here. Maybe we should think of waiting on God less as passively sitting around until something happens and more as actively attending—listening carefully for God's voice and watching intently for evidence of His moving in our lives and in the world around us.

Now, believe me, I understand that those of you reading these words who are in the midst of waiting for a miracle or waiting for a dream to be realized or waiting to be delivered from a dark, scary place probably feel helpless. You feel as if you're doing nothing, but you're actually doing something very important. In fact, this waiting—this attending to God—may be the most important spiritual work you could possibly do. While you are waiting faithfully on God, you are also allowing your hope to grow up. And if you can't be still and wait and hope—even when you have no reason to hope—you can't become the person God created when He thought you into existence.

Spiritual transformation doesn't take place when we get what we want. It takes place while we're waiting. It is forged in us while we're waiting, hoping, and trusting, even though we have yet to receive what we long for. Spiritual transformation happens in the waiting room.

Waiting also helps us learn the vital lesson that just because a dream is delayed doesn't mean it is denied. When we continue to hope patiently and place our trust in God and in His schedule—not ours—we begin to gain the type of long-range perspective that allows us to have peaceful souls, even when the storms of life are raging about us. With God, we can wait out the storm and see the sun breaking through the clouds. When we trust in Him, we will eventually see the rainbow and the rebirth of our hopes and dreams.

Jesus and Waiting

As we wait, we can take great comfort in the knowledge that God doesn't ask us to do anything He hasn't already done. God has, in fact, field-tested waiting and given us the perfect example to follow in Jesus Christ.

Henri Nouwen, in *A Spirituality of Waiting*, makes this point beautifully. He tells the story of being called to the bedside of a friend who had spent his life as a social activist, busily involved with caring for others. But now, this human dynamo was confined to a sickbed by the cancer ravaging his body. He confessed to Nouwen that he had no way to even think about his life. His entire self-identity had always been framed by *doing*, by actively working on behalf of others. How, he wanted to know, could he understand his present circumstances in a way that didn't lead to despair?

Nouwen wisely answered this anguished question by pointing his friend to the last days of Jesus' life—the period Christians often refer to as Christ's Passion. Up until this point in His life, Jesus' ministry had consisted largely of doing: healing, teaching, confronting, comforting, and actively modeling the God-life for all those He met. But when He was arrested by the Temple police, He was forced into a time of waiting. Nouwen wrote:

> The central word in the story of Jesus' arrest is one I never thought much about. It is "to be handed over."... Some translations say that Jesus was "betrayed," but the Greek says he was "handed over." Judas handed Jesus over (see Mark 14:10). But the remarkable thing is that the same word is used not only for Judas but also for God. God did not spare Jesus, but handed him over to benefit us all (see Romans 8:32)....
>
> [I]mmediately after Jesus is handed over, he becomes the one to whom things are being done. He's being arrested; he's being led to the high priest; he's being taken before Pilate; he's being crowned with thorns; he's being nailed on a cross. Things are being done to him over which he has no control....
>
> Jesus does not fulfill his vocation in action only but also in passion. He doesn't just fulfill his vocation by doing the things the Father sent him to do, but also by letting things be done to him that the Father allows to be done to him.... In a

way, his agony is not simply the agony of approaching death. It is also the agony of having to wait.[1]

In other words, even Jesus, God-in-the-flesh, had to endure waiting in order to fulfill His greatest purpose. In the same way, as we wait in faith upon God, we become more like Christ in His perfect obedience, His perfect sacrifice.

The apostle Paul underlined this truth when he said, in Philippians 3:10 and 11, "I want to know Christ—yes, to know the power of his resurrection and participation in his sufferings, becoming like him in his death, and so, somehow, attaining to the resurrection from the dead." Paul knew there was no shortcut to resurrection. If Christ had to pass through the gate of suffering in order to arrive at resurrection, then Paul wanted to walk the same path.

How Long Do You Wait?

At the center of our struggle with waiting is the conflict between our timeline and God's. Because we are limited by our perspective as time-bound creatures, we will never be able to grasp the vast difference between how we view the events in our lives and how God views them.

In John 11, the Bible tells about a man named Lazarus who became very sick. Lazarus was the brother of Mary and Martha, and the three of them were very good friends of Jesus and faithful supporters of His ministry. Indeed, when Jesus was passing through Bethany, their hometown, He was often the house guest of Lazarus and his sisters.

When Jesus heard of His friend's serious illness, He reacted a bit strangely. Instead of rushing to Lazarus's bedside, the Bible says Jesus stayed where He was for two more days. And by the time He finally arrived in Bethany at Lazarus's house, Lazarus was dead.

Now, the thing that is even more disturbing about this is that Jesus soon tells His followers that He knows Lazarus is dead. Not only that, but He tells them He is glad He wasn't there when the death happened. He says to them, "For your sake I am glad I was not there, so that you may believe" (John 11:15). In other words, Jesus says the death of Lazarus would serve some larger purpose; it was somehow going to contribute to the strengthening of His disciples' faith.

Can you imagine how Mary and Martha might have felt about this? Well, actually, you don't have to imagine it, because in John 11:21 and 32 the Bible records the words of first, Martha, and then Mary, when Jesus arrived at their house: "If you had been here, [our] brother would not have died."

Have you ever felt like Mary and Martha? Have you ever been in the waiting room, hoping for God to show up, but He doesn't? Sometimes God waits for two days. Sometimes, He waits for two years. We can't understand why He hasn't come, why we are still stuck in the waiting room.

Of course, the end of the story is that Jesus raised Lazarus from the dead, even though he had already been in the tomb for four days. And the result was a great demonstration of

God's power that caused many people to believe in Jesus as the Messiah. But when Jesus arrived in Bethany, Mary and Martha—and Jesus' disciples, for that matter—couldn't see any of this. They had no idea Jesus had a greater purpose in mind. All they knew was that Lazarus, their friend and brother, was dead and that Jesus could have prevented it by getting there sooner.

I do love something Martha says to Jesus, even in the midst of her grief at the passing of her brother. After she tells Jesus that He could have prevented Lazarus's death by getting there sooner, she says, "But I know that even now God will give you whatever you ask" (John 11:22). Even in her grief, Martha lets Jesus know that she still believes in Him, that she still trusts in His ability to provide—even when she doesn't understand his timing.

I believe this is a key to the spiritual transformation that comes through faithful waiting: realizing that God's power is greater than our circumstances. When our trust is in the Maker of heaven and earth, we can realize that what matters most is not what is happening *to* us, but what is happening *in* us.

We have to face the fact that no matter how long, patiently, and faithfully we wait, our time in the waiting room will not always end with the result we hoped for. We all have experienced this. That's why it is so hard to wait. We know it may not turn out the way we want it to. But if we can wait in faith and hope—even when there seems to be no more reason for hope—then God can do things in our lives that are beyond anything we could have hoped for. These things may not look like anything we had envisioned or dreamed, but they will serve His greater purpose in a way we would have never imagined. That day in Bethany, nobody was expecting to see a resurrection. But that was what Jesus had in mind from the beginning.

Waiting and Life

So life isn't turning out exactly the way you thought, and you have laid it before God in prayer, over and over again. You've taken the steps you know to take and prepared yourself to the best of your ability—and it still isn't happening.

Is it time to move on? Is failure inevitable? And if it is, how much longer should you keep prolonging the obvious?

As I said earlier, my bias is that, most of the time, we give up too soon. I prefer to help people see all the possibilities God may be placing before them. I am always hesitant to place time limits on God. The important thing is to continue trusting the end result to God, even when the outcomes you want are not immediately apparent.

Remember that faithful waiting—attending—involves much more than passively sticking your hands up in the air until God rains blessings down into your palms. Faithful waiting involves actively seeking contentment, even amid less-than-optimal circumstances.

Can you listen for God's guidance, even when things aren't going your way? Can you proactively trust Him, even when you aren't seeing the evidence of the victory you long for?

I encourage you to keep doing the next right thing, taking

the steps you know to take, without getting frustrated because you aren't yet where you want to be. Act on the belief that God has a plan and that He is bringing it to completion in your life. Commit to being ready for that completion to occur, even if you can't see it coming.

Another thing that can help with waiting is to create space in your life for what I call "altars": tangible reminders of what God has done for you in the past. This is a principle that is well attested in the Old Testament. So many times, at pivotal points in the history of God's people, they would build an altar or raise a commemorative stone to remind them of God's great acts of deliverance. Usually, they would build the monument at or near the place where God's act occurred, as Jacob did at Bethel when God gave him the vision of the ladder going up to heaven, or as Joshua did at the crossing of the Jordan when Israel entered the Promised Land—when God miraculously parted the floodwaters to allow the people to cross.

Now, I'm not telling you to start stacking rocks in your front yard every time God answers a prayer. But maybe you could do something like what an author friend of mine did: he still has the letter from the publisher who agreed to produce and market his first book, more than thirty years ago. He keeps that letter as a remembrance of God's act of blessing—as an altar. During the slow times, when the writing isn't going so well or when he can't seem to find the right place for his next project, he looks at that letter and remembers what God has done for him.

Maybe your altar is the deposit slip for a check that arrived unexpectedly but just at the right time to avoid a financial disaster. Maybe your altar is a framed copy of the Bible verse that encouraged you to try one more time—the time when you finally heard "yes." Maybe your altar is the ring your husband bought you when the two of you renewed your wedding vows after coming through a grueling trial in your marriage.

The point is, God has done mighty things in your life, and He will continue to do them, if you trust Him. Maybe some kind of tangible reminder could help you remember that if He did it before, He can do it again . . . you just have to keep waiting faithfully.

I also know that in the life of my church community, there have been times when our leadership team has recognized we have done all we can do as humans. The next step is completely up to God. When you arrive at a point like that in your own journey, realize that waiting upon God and trusting Him for the outcome is not the absence of something. Instead, it is the presence of spiritually transformative faith.

In every life, there are times of great forward motion, and there are times of waiting. Just as Christ, after acting so vigorously for much of His ministry, had to endure the agonizing wait of the Passion, so we must recognize and conform ourselves to the holy rhythm of waiting on God's timing. And who knows? It could be that you are only three days away from the resurrection.

Chapter Five in Review

Key Ideas

1. Often we desire God's power, but we aren't willing to accept God's calendar.
2. We don't get to see God at His most powerful unless we spend some time in the waiting room.
3. We live in a culture and a society that has done everything possible to eliminate the need for waiting.
4. While you are waiting faithfully on God, you are also allowing your hope to grow up.

Reflection Questions

1. Think of the people in your life whom you consider to have the deepest faith. What "waiting rooms" have these individuals experienced?
2. Do you consider yourself a patient person or an impatient person? How does this attribute (or its absence) usually look in your daily life?
3. Do you think of waiting as primarily a passive thing or as primarily an active thing? How can "doing the next right thing" be a form of waiting?

Your Next Step

Think of a time in your life when you were "in the waiting room." As you look back on that experience, write a note from yourself in the "here and now" to the person you were in the "there and then." Tell your past self what you have learned since that experience.

SIX

GIVE UP YOUR CONTAINER

*"We must be willing to let go of the life we have
planned, so as to have the life that is waiting for us."*
—E. M. Forster

The story of Abraham takes up a big chunk of Genesis, the first book in the Bible. Chapters 12 through 24 present the story of his life, starting with his call from God while he was still living with his father in Harran (an ancient city located in what we now call Turkey). God told Abraham to pack up all his belongings, leave behind his kin and all his friends, and head to a place God would show him when he got there. And Abraham (or Abram, as he was known at the time) obeyed.

No doubt, Abraham, as a young man from a fairly prosperous family in Ur, had a pretty good idea of how his life was going to look. And perhaps he was surprised when, one day, his father Terah announced that they were all relocating to Harran, a place far to the northwest of Ur (which was located in the southern part of what we now know as Iraq). Like many young people nowadays, Abraham and his young wife, Sarai (she would come to be known as Sarah), may have felt a bit sad to be pulling up stakes and leaving the well-watered plains bordering the Euphrates River, where Ur was located, to head off into the arid wilderness to the northwest. But Terah was the patriarch, and in those days, you did what the patriarch said.

The family caravan reached Harran, and they settled there. Though Harran was not nearly as cosmopolitan as Ur, it was still located on a major trade route, so it is likely that Terah and his clan could enjoy a measure of comfort in Harran.

But once again, God had other plans. Genesis 12:1 records His message to Abraham: "The Lord had said to Abram, 'Leave your country, your people and your father's household and go to the land I will show you.'"

God also promised to make of Abram a great nation (his new name, Abraham, means "father of nations"). He promised to bless and protect Abraham and promised that all the people on earth would be blessed through him.

So, although once again his life was being transformed into a shape he did not recognize or anticipate, Abraham took God at His word. He and his family headed southwest, toward a place called Canaan.

When the Container Changes

All of us have a picture in mind of how our lives will look. We have a container labeled "My Life" into which we pour all the hopes, intentions, and objectives that define the direction we intend for our lives to take.

What does *your* container look like? If you are still living at home with your parents, does your container feature a college degree and a job in your chosen field? Or are you an artist who longs to have the freedom to create, pursuing your muse wherever it leads you? Have you always dreamed of marriage and kids?

If you're a bit older, maybe your container features a steady career at the same company, followed by a comfortable retirement. Or maybe your container holds the future you have imagined for your grown children—one in which they are happily settled in their own homes, with perhaps a few grandchildren coming to your house for visits now and then.

But sometimes, the containers for our dreams change. Sometimes, as with Abraham, God has a different container in mind for us—one that doesn't look like the image we are familiar with. When this happens, we have to choose whether we will surrender—voluntarily trade in our container for the one God is offering us—or whether we will stubbornly cling to the way we had everything mapped out.

I don't think surrendering our plans to God means we give up on them. But I do believe we must keep our hearts open to the possibility that the container for our future won't always look the way we imagined it.

When God called Abraham to leave his family and head off to the place God would show him, He was asking Abraham to give up his preconceived ideas of how his life was going to look. God even articulates a dream for Abraham's life: "I will make you into a great nation." So, the dream is still there, but the container is looking very different.

Abraham was willing to trust God with the outcome. He was willing to say, in effect, "Here is my container. I give it to You freely. I will let You pour my dreams into a different container, and I will trust You for how it all turns out."

Surrendering the Outcome

This would not be the last time the shape of Abraham's container would shift. For one thing, though God had promised to make him into a great nation, Abraham and Sarah weren't able to have children.

When Abraham was ninety-nine years old and his wife was well into her eighties, God spoke to Abraham and told him that he and Sarah would have a son, according to God's promise to make him the father of a great nation. At this point, as one who was nearly a centenarian, Abraham had to be wondering how God was going to pull this off. In fact, the Bible says he laughed at the idea. I don't think he was laughing at God; I believe he was thinking about his age and frailty, and that of his wife, and trying to imagine the two of them as parents of a newborn. Sarah laughed, too, when she heard about it. You've got to admit; it's a pretty humorous image. But God was completely serious. And sure enough, about a year later, Abraham and Sarah walked down the hall from the geriatric ward into labor and delivery, and they welcomed into their home a bouncing baby boy whom they named Isaac—which, fittingly, means "laughter."

Once again, though Abraham thinks his life is going one direction, God sends him along a different path. Instead of sitting in their tent, studying brochures from retirement homes, he and Sarah are shopping for baby clothes and fixing up the nursery. I have never known a couple in their eighties and nineties who found out they were pregnant, but I have known some faithful people of God who suddenly found themselves with a much different container than the one they thought they would have.

Henri Nouwen was a brilliant thinker, teacher, and pastor. A Catholic priest, Nouwen had an outstanding career as a professor of psychology, pastoral ministry, spirituality, and social justice at prestigious universities such as Notre Dame and the divinity schools at Yale and Harvard. He wrote thirty-nine books, which have sold more than seven million copies and have been translated into more than thirty languages. Yet Nouwen reached a point in life when he felt adrift. In the midst of his confusion, he received a call to minister at Daybreak, a community in Richmond Hill, Ontario, that cared for adults with profound disabilities.

So, here was this brilliant theologian, pastor, psychologist, and scholar, spending his time with people who, in many cases, were neither able to hear or understand anything he said. In fact, Nouwen became the caretaker for Adam Arnett, a man who had such profound developmental challenges that Nouwen had to feed, bathe, and dress Adam every morning. He had to assist Adam in communicating. And yet, as Nouwen tells it, it was at Daybreak, helping to care for Adam, that he had his deepest, most transformational experiences of what it means to be beloved of God.

Some of Nouwen's most deeply spiritual and influential writing would flow out of his time at Daybreak. Yet, this container wasn't anything like the one he had originally envisioned for himself.

Sometimes, we have to surrender our plans, even in the midst of pursuing them. This doesn't mean we are giving up, just that we are handing over to God the responsibility for the outcome.

What Does It Mean to Surrender?

Usually, the word *surrender* has a negative connotation. It means we have been defeated; we are admitting that another person, entity, or situation has bested us. Surrender means giving up, waving the white flag.

But *surrender* can have another, more affirmative meaning. Instead of the connotation of becoming passive and admitting failure, as with defeat in battle, to surrender can carry the meaning of acceptance of a higher good or of receiving into one-self the will of a higher power. Seen in this light, surrendering to God's desires for our lives does not mean we are defeated by Him. Instead, it means that we choose to ally ourselves and our purposes with His greater purpose. This type of surrender is the *opposite* of defeat. When we surrender to God, He gives us the victory.

Abraham's Final Test

It might seem that once Abraham saw the birth of his son that he would pretty much be on cruise control from that point forward. After all, the man was a hundred years old! Surely by this point, he is ready for a well-deserved retirement and no more surprises, right?

Apparently not, according to God. Genesis 22:2 records it: "Then God said, 'Take your son, your only son, whom you love—Isaac—and go to the region of Moriah. Sacrifice him there as a burnt offering on a mountain I will show you.'"

Excuse me? Did I read that correctly? God has gone to all the trouble to help Abraham get a son—after promising to make Abraham the father of a great nation—and now He is telling Abraham to kill the boy? Are we missing something here?

I'm afraid not. And apparently Abraham was in no doubt, either, because the very next words in the Bible are, "Early the next morning Abraham got up and loaded his donkey." No hesitation. God says it, and Abraham gets up to go do it.

Many of us know that, in the end, God will not allow Abraham to slaughter his son and burn his remains. God wanted to see just how deep Abraham's faith really was—whether he would accept the strange and frightening shape of this new container God was offering him. God stays Abraham's hand, even as he is about to plunge the knife into Isaac, and directs Abraham to offer a ram instead—one that is conveniently caught in some nearby brambles.

But Abraham's surrender to God was complete. As the Bible explains elsewhere, "Abraham reasoned that God could even raise the dead, and so in a manner of speaking he did receive Isaac back from death" (Hebrews 11:19). In other words, Abraham trusted God so much that he believed God was stronger than death.

Because of the total surrender of his container—in this case, a container shaped like his son Isaac—Abraham became known as "the father of the faithful." By giving up control of the container to God, Abraham received the final victory.

Who Is Flying the Airplane?

Such radical surrender does not come easily. It requires facing down the toughest enemy most of us will ever know: our own desire for control.

I know a young professional who has a real struggle with flying. Actually, he isn't afraid of flying, per se, but of flying on a commercial airliner.

He said once, "I could fly anywhere on a small, private plane and have no problem whatsoever, because I know that if something were to happen, I could get to the pilot's seat and take control of the airplane.

"But on a commercial jet? The pilot and copilot are locked behind a bulkhead. I'm out of control. And it makes me crazy."

Do you hear what this young man is saying? Now, mind you, he is not a licensed pilot. As far as I know, he has never flown an aircraft in his life. And yet, his need for control is so deep-seated that even as his rational mind is telling him that he doesn't know how to fly an airplane, his emotions are telling him that he is better off being in control—or having the potential to be in control.

While few of us have to wrestle with such an extreme form of this fear, we all must deal with our need for control of our lives. Like the young man in the story above, we often crave control, even while knowing, in our heart of hearts, that we don't really know what we're doing.

By surrendering to God, however, we are offering up control to the only Being in the universe who always, absolutely, in every circumstance, knows what He is doing. As 1 John 3:20 says, "God is greater than our hearts, and he knows everything." No matter what you are facing and no matter how bewildering, scary, sad, or dangerous it is, God knows what needs to happen. By handing your container over to Him, trusting that He is in control, you will see blessing poured into your life. The container you get back may not look the same, but you can rest assured it is holding God's future for you—your destiny.

"What Is God's Will for My Life?"

This may be the all-time, number-one question that pastors get asked. And it may also be the most difficult one to answer. Because the fact is that all too often, the person is really asking God to bless his or her chosen container, instead of the one God is shaping.

I will say that one thing I've noticed about God's plan for any particular person's life is that it is just about impossible to define. And that makes sense, because just as each of us is a unique individual, different from everybody else right down to our fingerprints, God has a unique plan for each of us. But we do sometimes get some hints.

God's will for you can be as simple as an idea that somehow stays in your mind without any particular effort on your part. It can be as faint as an inkling or as strong as a deep passion. It can come on you all at once, or it can grow in you a little at a time, until suddenly you realize it is something you must pursue.

I've known a few people who can point to an event as dramatic as that of Paul on the road to Damascus—a sudden, blinding moment when everything became clear and God's call was as obvious as the color of their shirts. But these cases are the exception. For most of us, God's calling in our lives is a desire, a hope, or even a cluster of interests that just feels natural to us.

It would be easy, while contemplating God's plan for you and trying to determine what it might be, to fall victim to what golfers call "paralysis by analysis." Some people peer into themselves with a microscope, searching for God's will. I think that's the wrong approach. If you're having trouble figuring out God's purpose, God isn't the one who is hiding it from you. He's the one who put it inside you in the first place!

There is tremendous freedom in our journey with God. Instead of navel-gazing in search of God's purpose, I believe we ought to be gazing at the face of God. Psalm 37:4 tells us, "Take delight in the LORD, and he will give you the desires of your heart." As I said at the beginning of this book, the One who created us has hardwired us for the desire to fulfill our destinies. Jesus has promised us that anyone who longs to know God's will for her life will be able to find it because "everyone who asks receives; the one who seeks finds; and to the one who knocks, the door will be opened" (Matthew 7:8).

Practical Tips

There are some other things you can do to get a handle on your purpose. Always first, as outlined above, is to earnestly seek God in prayer, asking for knowledge of His purpose for your life. But you can also find someone whom you trust and whose faith you admire—someone who, in your estimation, is already living the dream God has placed in his heart. Chances are, this person has a fair amount of spiritual discernment. Ask this individual his opinion of why God has placed you on the earth.

You can also do this thought experiment: If someone suddenly gave you a financial fortune, what would you do? The answer probably has something to do with your life's purpose.

Now, if you say, "Move to a tropical island and sip pink drinks," you are probably mistaking your dream for the ending of your stress. Go a step beyond that: When your stress is a thing of the past, what would you do *then* to seek meaning and fulfillment? Chances are, that's what God has put you on earth to accomplish.

Become a careful observer of your own life. Step back from yourself, and ask big-picture questions like these:

- What have I always been good at?
- What needs do I care about most?
- Whom do I most admire?
- What makes me feel most fulfilled?

However you choose to go about it, I strongly advise that you exercise great patience and trust as you carry out this search. Trying to grasp God's will for your life in all its completion and complexity is probably beyond the abilities of most of us. But I do believe it is possible for most of us to hear within our hearts God's call to take the next step, to do the next right thing. And after all, the most important step you can take is the one you need to take right now.

Most of the time, in fact, there will be an element of the unknown to our journey. You can bet that if God is involved, there is always going to be an aspect of mystery, because God is just too immense, too powerful, and too beautiful for our human minds to contain. So, if you still don't have God figured out and if you aren't yet sure about every detail of what He wants you to do with your life, you're in excellent company!

I also believe we need to be careful that we aren't projecting our dreams onto God. Too often, like those people I was talking about earlier, we come to God with our agendas and ask Him to give His stamp of approval. Or, as mentioned above, we want to over-define God's will so every minuscule detail is scrutinized beyond the point of sense. This is another area that calls for deep, searching prayer and lots of time spent walking hand-in-hand with God. It also helps to seek the wise counsel of the spiritual leaders God has placed in your life.

Let's face it: we are humans, and our thoughts, perceptions, feelings, and beliefs are neither foolproof nor fail-safe. When we seek to follow God's plan for our lives, we must always approach the journey with an attitude of humility, trusting God more than we trust ourselves. But we must also remember that God is good and patient and loving. He cherishes lives spent in honoring Him with our best efforts, whether we are preaching a sermon to a thousand people or repairing shoes for a customer as carefully as we would work on our own.

Do what God has placed in your heart to do, and do it the best you can, whether anyone is watching or not. That brings honor to God's name and a smile to His face. Or, as Paul says in Colossians 3:23 and 24, "Whatever you do, work at it with all your heart, as working for the Lord, not for human masters. . . . It is the Lord Christ you are serving."

Giving It Up, Every Day

Ultimately, living God's plan for your life means offering up your container every day—surrendering the shape of your plans, your hopes, and your desires to God. When the apostle Paul talks about this, he uses the language of sacrifice. He says, in Romans 12:1, "Therefore, I urge you, brothers and sisters, in view of God's mercy, to offer your bodies as a living sacrifice, holy and pleasing to God—this is your true and proper worship."

I heard someone once say the biggest problem with a living sacrifice is that it keeps crawling off the altar. This is true of all of us; we just can't stay put!

We keep forgetting that control—for humans, at least—is an illusion. That's right: control is a myth. Even when I think I have it, I really don't.

But instead of seeing this as a negative, I can view it as a positive. Instead of focusing on my lack of control, I can be thankful for the constant flow of new experiences, ideas, and opportunities that are coming into my life. Instead of pleading for my old container or demanding that God restore it to its original shape, I can accept with thanksgiving the one He is placing in my hands, trusting that it will do a better job of holding the future He has prepared for me.

Let me tell you about my friend Tim. If anybody ever had a bead on how his life was going to turn out—from a pretty early age—it was Tim.

Tim's athletic gifts became apparent to lots of people, even when he was still a young kid. By the time he was in the fifth grade, he already knew that he was destined to play professionally. And when he got into high school and started playing football, people all over the state started to notice. Before long, Tim was All-Everything in his home state; he was a shoo-in for a full ride at a major university, and he wound up at Penn State.

Now, you have to understand that Tim is also a deeply humble man, one with deep spirituality. His success did not—as it does all too often—spoil his attitude. Instead, it made him want to work harder, to get better, to succeed more. He was truly driven to get stronger, faster, smarter.

By the time Tim was ready to graduate from college, the shape of his container was fairly well defined. Tim fully expected to be drafted into the National Football League and to have a fulfilling, productive career as a professional athlete. Given Tim's accomplishments, that was a more than reasonable expectation.

Sure enough, he was drafted in an early round by the Carolina Panthers—but he was cut at the end of the first season.

For the first time in his life, Tim realized that there was nothing he could do to keep his container intact. "All I could do was wait on God," he said.

Not long after that, he was picked up on waivers by the Jacksonville Jaguars—and cut the following September. Next, he played a season in Chicago, but was cut again.

Finally, the Tennessee Titans picked Tim up. He had a good year, even being selected as a Pro Bowl alternate. But for the past four years, he had played for four different teams. As

September neared, he realized that he was secretly dreading the phone call that would inform him he wouldn't be playing for the Titans the following season.

However, the phone call didn't come. In fact, at the beginning of Tim's second season as a Titan, he was voted by his fellow players as a captain of special teams. He had a good year the second year . . . and the third . . . and the fourth.

By this time, Tim says, he was starting to think that finally, things were going to work out as he had hoped since he was a fifth grader. He was going to have a good career with the Titans and pursue his life goals all the way to the end.

And then, at the end of his fourth season, the call came. Tim had been cut again. And this time, no one picked him up on waivers.

Of this time in his life, Tim said one of the most insightful things I've ever heard: "I realized that God was loosening my grip on the game." Tim said he realized that for a long while, he had been telling God how his life was supposed to go, instead of turning loose and letting God tell him.

My friend Tim made the difficult decision to retire from professional football at the age of thirty—a time when he had all reasonable expectation of having several good seasons left. But he realized that he had to give up control of the shape of the container holding God's plan for his life. Tim's faith and his surrender to God's will continue to inspire me and everyone else who knows him.

One of the blessings of God's eternal perspective on our lives is that He does not define us as we define ourselves.

God does not view us as the outcome of our efforts—whether they are successful or not. Instead, He is more interested in whether we are living as faithful, trusting, obedient children.

I often think about Jeremiah, the Old Testament prophet. If Jeremiah had to give a report to his missions committee or his evangelism board, what would he say?

"Jeremiah, how many converts did you win this week?"

"Well . . . none, I guess."

"Jeremiah, did you convince the king to stop doing evil things?"

"Umm . . . no, I don't think so."

"Jeremiah, has anyone paid any attention whatsoever to your preaching?"

"Not that I can tell, actually."

The way *we* judge things, Jeremiah was a colossal failure! And yet God did not view Jeremiah as a failure; He saw Jeremiah as faithful. Jeremiah lived a life of daily surrender, but he never gave up.

As a matter of fact, I think success is one of the most spiritually dangerous things we can encounter. If you think about it, most of the people in this world who are most likely to oppress others, to be prideful, or to be greedy are those who have been very successful, in one way or another.

You see, the problem with my success is that I—and the people around me—start to notice it. Pretty soon, I am getting all kinds of favorable attention and even deference from all quarters. I start getting invited to better parties. Big shots are asking me to sit on their boards of directors. And then, I start to believe my own press. When success is rolling in, I start to believe I am personally responsible for it. I start to believe I not only am entitled to this success but that I manufactured it without any help from anybody, thank you very much.

From there, it's only a short step to convincing myself that I don't really need God all that much. After all, what has He done for me lately?

Now, don't get me wrong; I'm not *anti*-success. And I happen to know a number of very godly, humble people who are also very successful. But these are people who have learned how to give up their containers, every day. They trust God for the next step, knowing that He is in charge, not them.

What does *your* container look like? Are you willing to hand it over to God? Remember, this doesn't mean you are giving up. It just means you are learning how to surrender. And when you've mastered the art of surrendering to God, that's when the real victory begins.

 Chapter Six in Review

Key Ideas

1. We have a container labeled "My Life" into which we pour all the hopes, intentions, and objectives that define the direction we intend for our lives to take.

2. Sometimes, we have to surrender our plans, even in the midst of pursuing them. This doesn't mean we are

giving up, just that we are handing over to God the responsibility for the outcome.

3. Surrendering to God's desires for our lives does not mean we are defeated by Him. Instead, it means we choose to ally ourselves and our purposes with His greater purpose.

4. For most of us, God's calling in our lives is a desire, a hope, or even a cluster of interests that just feels natural to us. In some way, it represents a vision of what we'd like to see our lives become.

5. God does not view us as the outcome of our efforts— whether they are successful or not. Instead, He is more interested in whether we are living as faithful, trusting, obedient children.

Reflection Questions

1. Do you view success more as a blessing or more as a danger? Why do you think it is difficult for some people to properly handle success?

2. As you reflect on your life so far, has the shape of your container changed? If it has, how did you react? If it hasn't, how do you think you would react if it did?

3. On a scale from 1 to 10, with "1" being "I ask God about everything I do, even the smallest decisions," and "10" being "I ask God about the big decisions, but I trust myself with the day-to-day stuff," where would you rate yourself?

Your Next Step

For the next four days, ask yourself one of these questions each day:

- What have I always been good at?
- What needs do I care about most?
- Whom do I most admire?
- What makes me feel most fulfilled?

After thinking quietly about each day's question, offer it to God in prayer, asking that His will, not yours, be done.

SEVEN

ENDURE THE DIP

*"[W]hile others celebrated she walked slowly homeward,
seeing life in a new and painful clarity: with different
gods, her husband . . . would have been a different man."*
—James Michener, *The Source*

Some of the most powerful words in the Bible are very near the beginning. In Genesis 1:26, the Bible says, "Then God said, 'Let us make mankind in our image, in our likeness.'"

Take a moment to allow that idea to soak in. The Creator of the universe had the stated desire to make humankind *in His image*! It was God's specific purpose to fashion us with the stamp of His identity, His nature. We are bearers of the divine character!

In the Genesis account, the creation of humankind is the last item on God's agenda. It receives the prominence of the capstone, the crowning achievement of creation. We read in Genesis 2:1–2 that when God had created humans—male and female—in His image and had blessed them, it was the completion of His work of creation. After this was done, He rested.

This means that every single person you see—from the homeless woman panhandling on the corner to the movers and shakers in high-rise office suites—carries within a spark of the divine Spirit of God. As C. S. Lewis says in *The Weight of Glory*, "You have never talked to a mere mortal. Nations, cultures, arts, civilizations—these are mortal, and their life is to ours as the life of a gnat."[1] Every single human being who lives, who has ever lived, or who will ever live possesses an immortal spirit that carries the indelible stamp of the Creator of the heavens and the earth.

In a recent post on catalystspace.com titled "Kings and Priests," John Ortberg wrote, "In ancient Mesopotamian culture, only kings were made in the image of a powerful god; peasants were actually thought to be made by inferior gods."[2] He goes on to explain how the Genesis account challenges this idea: we are *all* made in the image of the supreme God; we *all* carry a splinter of His nature within ourselves. In fact, the main reason God has placed us on the earth is to be tiny versions of Him—little mirrors that reflect to others the image of God within us. When we imitate our Creator, we bring glory to Him and blessing to everything and everyone around us.

When the Mirror Goes Dark

Too often, we do a poor job of imitating the One whose image we bear. According to the Bible, God breathed His own breath—His own life—into us, but much of the time, what we breathe back out is not blessing but selfishness, hatred, and anger. Instead of reflecting God, we are reflecting our own desires and fears.

Distorted images of God lead to distorted lives. Like the pagan worshiper in the quote at the beginning of this chapter, our gods determine who we are. If we worship something other than the true God—usually, something we have dressed up and named "god"—our lives will reflect the degraded substitute instead of the actual glory of God.

Distorted views of God also lead to destructive attitudes and behaviors. Many eating disorders, for example, are rooted in an unhealthy need for control. People who manipulate and abuse others do not worship God but their own appetites and ambitions. Those who see God as a punitive, harsh, unforgiving taskmaster are apt to treat others the same way.

A few years ago, the movie *Stand and Deliver* told the powerful story of Jaime Escalante, a math teacher at one of the toughest high schools on LA's east side. Instead of accepting the fact that his students were gang-bangers, destined for a short, violent life, Escalante challenged them to learn math, insisting that this was their ticket out of the barrio—if they chose to use it.

Progress was slow at first, but a few kids agreed to enroll in algebra. Escalante pushed them to achieve, and many of them responded. He put in place high expectations for them, and students began to meet them. After four years at the school and after persuading a reluctant school administration, Escalante began offering advanced placement calculus classes. Two of the five students in his first class passed the AP exam at the end of the course. Within three years, fourteen of the fifteen students in the class passed the exam. The next year, eighteen passed. The year after that, thirty passed.

At the height of Escalante's career, students from his east LA high school were entering the University of Southern California in larger numbers than students from all other east LA high schools combined. Many students from his school also were accepted into other California universities. Hundreds of students went on to become successful in their educations and subsequent careers, simply because Jaime Escalante looked at them and saw something besides poverty-stricken, culturally deprived, dangerous kids. Because he believed in them, they came to believe in themselves. He held up a mirror that allowed them to see clearly what they could become. Jaime Escalante not only gave his students permission to dream; he showed them a path toward making their dreams happen.

Many of us could tell similar stories about an influential teacher or other mentor. It makes a tremendous difference in your life when someone you respect believes in you. It causes you to reach for your better self. It allows you to see yourself in a different light.

Now, consider the truth that the Maker of heaven and earth believes *in you*! He sees you for who you really are, not who life has convinced you that you are. You carry His image; it is stamped in your soul. And that means the desires you carry within you are much more than idle wishes. They are there because of God's spirit. They are a part of His image that you carry.

That is why it is so important to see clearly, not in a blurred, distorted mirror. We were created to shine with God's light, to light our own way and to light the way for others.

The spirit of this world—our enemy, the devil—wants to deceive us. He wants to change the angle of the mirror so that, instead of reflecting the image of God, it shows us the problems, the shortcomings. Or he wants to turn our focus inward, to our failures and fears or to our self-centered aims and desires. He wants to do anything possible, in fact, to distract us from gazing at God. If he can keep our attention diverted— by worry, fear, greed, pride, or selfishness—he can cause us to believe we're on our own. He can separate us from the true Source of life, power, and blessing.

Getting Past the Dip

Management and marketing guru Seth Godin wrote a little book titled *The Dip*. In this clever look at persistence and its importance to success, he uses "the dip" to signify the phenomenon that often happens to us when the "new" wears off of whatever we're attempting to do—learning to play guitar, mastering another language, taking on a more challenging job, or whatever else you try. He describes an experience familiar to most of us. At first, the new thing is exciting and fun. We're motivated by the variety of the untried, and we take on the challenge enthusiastically. And then . . . we get stuck. We are no longer making progress as quickly as we were at first. In fact, it seems to be getting harder. Although the goal is worthwhile and important to us, it looks like it's getting farther away instead of closer.

This downturn is *the dip*. But this, Godin says, is exactly the place we have to be if we want to succeed. Most people, you see, will quit when they reach the dip. Those few who don't quit, however—the ones who persevere and make it past the dip—are the ones who set themselves apart.

When you're on the upside of the dip, the field is suddenly much less crowded. This is where success becomes more likely. I think the dip is where we learn to reflect the image of God most clearly. When we hang on through the tough times and don't give up, I believe God's image shines a little brighter for everyone around.[3]

This has never been proven any more powerfully than it was by the early Christians. Near the end of the second century A.D. and again about the middle of the third century, terrible plagues swept through Rome. The first, often called the Antonine Plague, after Marcus Aurelius Antoninus, one of the rulers during the period, broke out in about 165. It was probably either smallpox or measles, brought back to Rome by soldiers returning from a campaign in the eastern part of the empire. The second, usually referred to as the Plague of Cyprian (after Cyprian, the Bishop of Carthage), erupted around 251.

At their height, these pandemics were claiming as many as five thousand lives per day in Rome and even in the provinces, as far away as Egypt. Whole villages and even cities were abandoned. Some historians suggest that as much as a third of the population of Rome perished.

Panic set in. People fled Rome in droves, hoping to save their own lives. Contemporary chroniclers relate horrific scenes: families tossing infected, but still living, members into the street in an effort to avoid contracting the disease; piles of unburied dead everywhere because the general populace were too afraid to perform the final services for those who had died. But the Christians responded differently. At the urging of their leaders, they cared tenderly, not only for their own sick but for their pagan neighbors and friends, too. Often becoming infected themselves, they nevertheless ministered to the sick, the dying, and the dead. Here is how Dionysius, a bishop of the church in Alexandria, described it in a letter written about A.D. 260:

> Most of our brother Christians showed unbounded love and loyalty, never sparing themselves and thinking only of one another. Heedless of danger, they took charge of the sick, attending to their every need and ministering to them in Christ, and with them departed this life serenely happy; for

they were infected by others with the disease, drawing on themselves the sickness of their neighbors and cheerfully accepting their pains.[4]

These Christians willingly put themselves at risk because they believed that was what Jesus expected of them when He said, "Do unto others as you would have them do unto you."

And people noticed. In A.D. 362, the emperor Julian, in an effort to bring about a revival of the Roman pagan religion to counteract the rising tide of Christianity, attempted to set up a benevolent campaign among the adherents to paganism. He wrote in a letter to one of the high priests of a temple in the province of Galatia:

> I think that when the poor happened to be neglected and overlooked by the priests, the impious Galileans [Julian's term for Christians] observed this and devoted themselves to benevolence. . . . The impious Galileans support not only their poor, but ours as well . . . everyone can see that our people lack aid from us.[5]

Many scholars believe that one of the principal reasons for the rapid spread of Christianity in the early history of the church is the profound impact these believers exerted upon society by their self-sacrificing love. Even the emperors began to realize the Christian faith was irresistible. Nothing is as powerful as the image of God shining forth in the lives of His faithful people!

Ancient kings used to set up images of themselves in public places. They also used to impress their likeness on the coins people used for daily commerce. Why do you suppose they did that? It's pretty simple: they wanted to remind everyone in the kingdom of who was in charge. They intended for the kingdom's citizens to carry their image in mind at all times.

Like the ancient kings who stamped their images on coins, God has stamped His image on us. And His image not only indicates our eternal worth, it also reminds us of our destiny. We are citizens of His kingdom, bearers of His likeness.

Most of us will never go through a dip anywhere near as severe as the plagues of the ancient Roman Empire. But all of us will face tough times—days, weeks, months, or even years— when the thrill is gone, the way ahead seems steep and rocky, and we are wondering where we went wrong. In the pursuit of our life's goals, resistance is not necessarily a sign you are going in the wrong direction; it is often a sign that you are moving forward.

Find Meaning in the Struggle

I have never been what you would call proficient at the ancient and honorable game of chess, but I am fascinated by it all the same. I'm amazed at the skill and intellect required to see not only your next move, but your opponent's next move, and the next five or six moves after that. It boggles my mind.

One of the things I especially love about chess is the role of the pawns, those pieces lined up in the front row—cannon fodder for the fast-moving rooks, knights, and bishops. Because they can only move one space at a time and only in the forward direction, many players think of pawns as weak and valueless. They can be sacrificed with no great consequence. But some players, I've heard, jealously protect their pawns. They guard them carefully, saving them for the later stages of the game.

Why? Because if you can keep a pawn alive long enough to get it to the opponent's back row, the lowly pawn can be transformed into a queen, the most potent piece on the board.

To me, that is the essence of enduring the dip. When the going gets hard and you feel like a pawn, shuffling slowly from space to space, that's the time to hang in there! For all you know, you may be almost to the finish line. You may be just about to get your promotion, your spot in the limelight.

And it is a fact that, to God, you are not a pawn. You are made in His image, born to be an agent of His unfolding design for the world. Even when things look dark and you are questioning all your most basic assumptions, there is a divine spark in you that nothing can quench. God has invested you with meaning, with a purpose that nothing can take away.

Viktor Frankl was a neurologist and psychiatrist who practiced in Vienna, Austria, until 1942, when he and his family were deported to the Theresienstadt ghetto by the Nazis. Subsequently, Frankl was transferred to Dachau while his wife Tilly was sent to Bergen-Belsen, where she died.

Frankl endured the horror of the death camps, treating patients when he could. He spent five months as a slave laborer.

Somehow, he managed to survive until his camp was liberated by the Allies in 1945.

After the horror of the camps, Frankl pondered the meaning of his experiences. The ultimate outcome of his thinking would be captured in his profoundly influential book, *Man's Search for Meaning*, published in 1959. Frankl concluded that even under the cruelest conditions, life can still have meaning. Even suffering, he reasoned, can be an achievement if it is endured in the right way.

He relates a story of a forced march on a bitterly cold morning. The prisoner marching beside him commented, "I hope our wives are better off in their camps and don't know what is happening to us."[6] Frankl was suddenly captivated by the thought of his wife—his love for her and hers for him, the way she used to look at him, her kindness and understanding. He writes:

A thought transfixed me: for the first time in my life I saw the truth as it is set into song by so many poets, proclaimed as the final wisdom by so many thinkers. The truth—that love is the ultimate and the highest goal to which Man can aspire. Then I grasped the meaning of the greatest secret that human poetry and human thought and belief have to impart: *The salvation of Man is through love and in love.* I understood how a man who has nothing left in this world still may know bliss, be it only for a brief moment, in the contemplation of his beloved. . . . For the first time in my life I was able to understand the meaning of the words,

"The angels are lost in perpetual contemplation of an infinite glory."[7]

I believe Viktor Frankl was onto something. What he discovered on that frigid morning, in the midst of the most hopeless situation imaginable, is that even the worst times do not define the meaning of our lives. A loving God, who longs to walk with us and know us, has placed into us a portion of His own nature. And that—not our circumstances—is what defines us and sets us apart. That is what enables us to follow our dreams, even if we have to walk in the dark.

You were made to shine like a diamond. When you endure the dip and emerge on the other side, you will find that the experience has polished you to a harder, more durable glow. As you persist through the challenges, you will discover a bit more of the eternal spark placed in you by God.

 Chapter Seven in Review

Key Ideas

1. It was God's specific purpose to fashion us with the stamp of His identity, His nature. We are bearers of the divine character.
2. Distorted views of God lead to destructive attitudes and behaviors.
3. The dip is where we learn to reflect the image of God

most clearly. When we hang on through the tough times and don't give up, God's image shines a little brighter for everyone around.

Reflection Questions

1. Think of a time when you went through "the dip" and came out successfully. How did you feel when you were in the dip? How did it feel when you were looking back at it?
2. Why is it so important to know that someone else believes in us? Are there people in your life who need for you to believe in them? How can you show them that you do?
3. Think of some athletes who have performed well under pressure. What enables them to do this? Why do we value people—in all walks of life—who can do this?
4. Do you think there are times when persistence is ill-advised? How do you differentiate between "enduring the dip" and beating a dead horse?

Your Next Step

Eleanor Roosevelt said, "You must do the thing you think you cannot do."[8] What is something that scares you? Pick something; then go out and do it. Here are some suggestions:

- If you are shy, strike up a conversation with a stranger.
- If you are addicted to social media, spend one whole day without logging on with your phone, tablet, or computer.

- If you are protective of your possessions, give away something important to you.
- If you are mad at somebody, take the initiative to repair the relationship.
- If you see something unfair going on, speak up to someone in charge.

EIGHT

RECALIBRATE

*"You do not have to do these things—unless
you want to know God. They work on you, not
on him. You do not have to sit outside in the
dark. If, however, you want to look at the stars,
you will find that darkness is necessary."*
—Annie Dillard

Here's something I didn't know until recently: in centuries past, there was no standard tuning pitch for musical instruments. It varied from place to place, and sometimes, even from street to street within the same city.

"What difference would that make?" you may ask. Well, if you've ever gone to an orchestra concert, you might remember that the first thing that happens is the first-chair violinist, or concertmaster, walks out on stage (people usually clap; I'm not sure why). Then, the oboe player sounds a note. Next, the entire orchestra plays the same note, then different notes, as each performer makes sure his or her instrument is in sync with the tuning note. Once everybody is in tune, the conductor walks out (people clap again, even though nobody has really done anything yet), and soon the music begins.

It just so happens that the pitch the oboist plays for the tuning note is the A above middle C. To be precise, it is the A that is produced by 440 vibrations per second. Musicians usually call it *A 440*. If you go to a concert in Nashville, New York City, Berlin, Istanbul, or Tokyo, the orchestras will all tune to A 440. It is the modern standard concert pitch.

The advantage of this is that, if you are a musician, no matter where you go in the world, you can play with other musicians and know that you will all be in tune (well, as long as everyone is paying attention). If you are a trumpet player from Chicago and you are performing as a guest artist with the Budapest Festival Orchestra, your instrument will blend with the rest of the group. All of you are calibrated to the same standard.

Now, can you start to see the problem musicians were having a few centuries ago? There was no universally accepted standard. Each musician could do his or her own thing—which was a real difficulty if they wanted to perform together. The problem was compounded by the fact that musical instrument makers started to realize that the higher they pitched their instruments, the brighter and more brilliant the sound.

The problem got so bad that in the seventeenth century, a

German composer named Michael Praetorius reported that singers were straining their voices and strings were snapping on violins and lutes, as musicians tried to match their tuning with a "standard" that kept creeping higher and higher.

Getting on the Same Page

Just as any musician knows that his or her instrument needs to be recalibrated to A 440 before any important session or performance, we need to know that our lives have to be recalibrated on a regular basis. We need to measure ourselves against the standard, and God has provided us the perfect tuning pitch to make sure we are living in tune with the way He has designed us to function.

Proverbs 9:10 says, "The fear of the LORD is the beginning of wisdom, and knowledge of the Holy One is understanding." The Maker of heaven and earth, our Creator, is our standard. Because we are made in His image, our truest identity is found in Him. There is a holy rhythm involved when we are living in concert with God's dream for our lives.

But how do we recalibrate ourselves to God? How do we find that rhythm, so that we can, as Paul advised, "keep in step with the Spirit" (Galatians 5:25)?

The first step, as the writer of Proverbs suggests, is to fear God. This is not the type of fear that paralyzes or that results from anxiety about bodily or emotional harm. Instead, the fear of the Lord moves us. It inspires us to align ourselves with the only true standard, the One we were created to calibrate to.

We have to remind ourselves, over and over again, that we are part of a much larger story. We are, as Paul says in Greek, God's *poema*—His handiwork, His ongoing composition (Ephesians 2:10). We are characters in the grand story that God started when He said, "Let there be light"—the story that will be continued for eternity, long after the earth is dissolved and we have been gathered to the never-ending joy of heaven.

But—and this is a very important point—you and I are not the main characters in the story. God has the central part. He has written Himself into the narrative. And when we forget this and start to think the story is really about us, things stop making sense. Let me say it a different way: as long as you think you are the central character in the story, you are out of calibration. You're playing out of tune.

"I Will Be with You"

Many of our struggles with fear, in fact, arise from this same source: being out of calibration with God. We have placed ourselves—our challenges, our desires, our hopes, our plans, our anxieties—in the foreground. The problem with this is that it automatically puts God in the background, and He doesn't belong there. God is the lead character; He is not in a supporting role.

One of the most consistent assurances in Scripture is God's promise: "I will be with you." Over and over again, He tells His people that He will never abandon or forsake them.

The problem is, God's people are neither as faithful nor as consistent as He is. Repeatedly in the Bible, God pronounces His displeasure when His people begin placing their trust in their own efforts, rather than in Him.

Too often, we do the same thing. When we come up against life's challenges, we shove God into the background. Our own preoccupations become most important to us, rather than the recognition of God's constant presence and provision. We start trying to manage things for ourselves. Our fear skews our vision; we attempt to occupy a position in the universe to which we aren't entitled.

Instead of resting in God's presence, we are busy trying to do damage control. We think that our anxieties and problems are too immediate, too urgent, to wait for God's attention.

This is folly, of course. We were never meant to be in charge of everything, and when we try to live this way, we get out of kilter. Before long, we are so busy trying to keep all the plates spinning that we couldn't hear God's voice even if we wanted to. His promised presence is of little benefit to us, because we've forgotten how to recognize it.

Another problem we have is that, especially when we are facing uncertain or fearful times, we have trouble "feeling" God's presence. Though we may know intellectually and theologically that God is there, we can't sense Him in a way that makes us feel empowered for the trials we are facing.

How can we remember, even when everything seems to be falling apart, that God is with us? How can we recapture that pure, peaceful trust in God's presence that can support us even amid the storms of life?

We can purposefully, proactively discipline ourselves to recognize God's presence. We can re-sensitize ourselves to sense His love and His provision in our lives. We can recalibrate.

Staying in Alignment

Here's something interesting about calibration: we only need it for the most important things. This is what I mean: if you're helping the kids build a backyard fort out of scrap lumber, precise measurement—which is a form of calibration against a standard— isn't all that crucial. You pound in a few nails, prop it up on the side, and as long as it doesn't fall down, you don't worry about it. You know this isn't something that has to be built to last.

But if you were building a new house, would you hire a builder who didn't measure carefully? Would it be okay with you if the walls weren't plumb and the ceiling joists were of different lengths and angles?

When something is meant to last, it needs to be calibrated. You don't calibrate a disposable razor or a toothpick. When you're finished with it, you throw it away. But people aren't disposable. We are intended to live eternally, and this demands that we be calibrated against the standard of our

Maker, over and over again. Otherwise, we will end up living at cross-purposes with our destiny.

I've learned the hard way that proper alignment is important. Automobile tires aren't cheap, but I've worn out a set or two of tires prematurely because I didn't keep my car in alignment.

The trouble is that you can get used to poor alignment, can't you? You notice that the car seems to want to drift to the right when you're driving down the road, but you just compensate a little to the left with the steering wheel, and everything seems pretty much okay. But there's a price to be paid. Poor wheel alignment causes uneven tread wear on your tires, and sooner or later, you're going to have to do something about it. If you're lucky, you don't find out by way of a blowout; but at the very least, you're going to be springing for a new tire or two, long before it's really necessary.

In the same way, when our lives are out of alignment with God, it causes unnecessary wear and tear. Oh, we can acclimate, to a certain extent, and it may even be a long time before we realize the damage that has been done, but the damage is there. I see it in the eyes of people who come to me for counseling. It shows up in depression, in estranged family members, in ruined marriages, in broken friendships—in lost dreams.

We are not designed to live our lives out of alignment with God. If we don't periodically recalibrate, something, somewhere is going to get out of whack. And the consequences can be devastating.

What Causes Poor Alignment?

Because we live in a world marred by sin, there are many ways we can drift out of proper alignment with God's purpose for our lives. One of most pervasive causes of poor alignment is the wearying effect of time. Day in and day out, we face an endless stream of demands, desires, pressures, deadlines, duties, and expectations. We get tired. We lose focus.

There is a sort of natural drift that happens in our lives over time. We see it in every aspect of our existence, from the mundane to the extraordinary. We start to take things for granted; we get sloppy about the fundamentals; we start to cut corners.

This past summer I had the incredible opportunity to visit the world famous Lambeau Field, home of the Green Bay Packers. Now, I'm a Tennessee Titans fan through and through, but the opportunity to visit a place with so much history was a real treat. My boys got to run out of the players' tunnel to the sound of tens of thousands of fans (there wasn't actually anyone there; they just pumped the sound in over the stadium loudspeakers).

We got to walk around, soaking up all the cool history and stories about the different players and coaches who have been a part of this beloved franchise.

I love the story about Vince Lombardi during the years he coached the Green Bay Packers and fashioned them into a team that would win five NFL championships and the first two Super Bowls. Every year, on the first day of summer training camp, he would assemble the team. He would hold up a pigskin and say, "Gentlemen, this is a football." This was Lombardi's way of reminding these professional athletes that no one is ever too good to work on the basics.

It's the same way in our lives. If we don't build in times of recalibration—of renewal, resetting ourselves to the standard—we risk drifting gradually into spiritual carelessness and apathy. We lose our connection to the authentic. And perhaps most vital, when we encounter those soul-shaking times of trial and fear, we won't be conditioned to sense God's constant, comforting presence.

Another reason we get out of alignment is negative influences from the people around us. It's astounding how often negative people will try to rent space in your head. Don't let them, or you'll become one of them. We often underestimate the impact of the words we hear others say and the attitudes they express. Over time, negative and spiritually unaware speech and actions can have a dulling effect on our own spiritual focus.

This is why the community of faithful people is so important. We need each other! We need to get together—more often than just at church, by the way—in order to remind each other that we are still believing, still trying to stay properly aligned, still traveling the road toward God's dreams for us. We need, as Paul said, to "encourage one another and build each other up" (1 Thessalonians 5:11) so that we can all keep going down the road together.

The success and failure in our lives also gets us out of alignment. And honestly, I believe that success causes more alignment problems for me than failure. Why? Because when

I succeed, I can easily persuade myself that I did it all on my own. It is pretty easy for most of us to convince ourselves that we are, after all, pretty hot stuff!

When we fail, on the other hand, we are more likely to lean on others for support and encouragement to get up and try again. Failure teaches us that we are incomplete in ourselves. Failure helps us learn humility, which in turn makes us more apt to receive coaching, constructive criticism, and advice.

So, be wary of success! Remember the ancient Roman custom for generals returning from a victorious campaign. As the four-horse chariot wound its way through the streets and the crowds shouted praise for the triumphant commander, a slave would ride in the chariot beside the general and continually whisper in his ear, "You are but a mortal; one day, you will die."

How Can We Recalibrate?

The people I have seen who are the most successful at staying calibrated to God's purpose are those who are conscious of the holy rhythm I referred to earlier. They are sensitive to the ebb and flow of life, and they have consciously built in seasons of spiritual discipline in order to realign themselves with God's dream for their lives.

I have long been deeply impressed by the spiritual wisdom represented in the Jewish calendar. For one thing, the Jewish day begins, not at sunrise, but at sunset. This means that, for faithful Jews, the new day begins with the coming of darkness and the quiet and solitude of sleep. There is something profoundly spiritual about consciously beginning with quiet and rest. There is a sense in which each day begins with renewal and with surrender.

When you look at our modern culture, though, you realize how little we seem to value quiet and solitude. In our ever-expanding demand for more choices and more on-demand services, almost everything nowadays is available 24/7. You can go to the grocery store at three o'clock in the morning; you can drown out the stillness of the night with an endless selection of cable TV channels or streaming video.

But this is not how we were meant to live. At the very beginning, when God created the universe, the Bible says He did all His work in six days, and on the seventh day, He rested. For that reason, the Jewish belief in *Shavuot*, or the Sabbath, holds that this is a day of rest and contemplation. It is another way we honor the divine spark within us, recalibrating ourselves to the standard of the One who made us in His image.

The fact is that human beings need regular times of quiet, rest, solitude, and reflection. We need to build "Sabbath" into our lives, not because we're trying to impress others with our spirituality or to make brownie points with God, but because this is how we are wired. When we ignore that, we get out of alignment—out of calibration.

Prayer is an aspect of Sabbath that helps us reconnect with God. The spiritual discipline of prayer is how we continue to walk hand-in-hand with the God who longs to be with us.

I realize you can pray anywhere—on the commute, pushing

your cart down the aisle at Walmart, sitting in your office. All those are excellent places to pray. But we also need times of focused, dedicated prayer. We need to periodically set ourselves apart—Jesus called it going into our "closet" (Matthew 6:6 KJV)—with no distractions, in order to pour our hearts out to God and listen carefully within our spirits for His answers. Whenever we discipline ourselves to do this, we are recapturing Sabbath in our lives. We are being recalibrated for the pursuit of God's dream for us.

I know one man who makes it a practice to pray his way through his morning jog. No, he isn't praying to be able to make it through the run! As he jogs through his neighborhood, he prays for the people living around him. He prays for his kids and grandkids. He prays for his wife and for people that he knows. And he opens up to God about his doubts, his challenges, and his dreams.

Another important spiritual discipline is the study and contemplation of God's Word. As I mentioned in an earlier chapter, we must not kid ourselves into believing we can know God intimately without paying close attention to what He has said through the inspired words in the Bible. The psalmist says, "How sweet are your words to my taste, sweeter than honey to my mouth!" (Psalm 119:103). God's Word really does nourish us like rich food. It provides our spirits with the building blocks of growth and shows us the way to real wisdom and maturity. And when the times of testing come, God's word bears witness in our hearts to His constant, abiding presence.

The Bible gives us a view of God's dealings with humanity—both positive and negative—for the last six thousand years or so. When I read the words of Scripture and see how the people in the Bible mess up—even some of those we consider heroes of the faith—it fills me with confidence that God might be able to use me, too.

The Bible shows me that the problems I'm dealing with and the spiritual and emotional struggles I'm going through are not really anything new. It's kind of surprising to realize how little human nature has changed in the last six thousand years!

The Bible also comforts me in times of desolation and sorrow. I know of a spiritual leader who presents a seminar called "The Psalms Can Save Your Life." He walks through the Psalms of lament with people who are feeling intense grief, fear, or doubt, showing them where the psalmist has traveled the same path, crying out in anguish to God.

When the psalmist groans in Psalm 13, "How long, LORD? Will you forget me forever? . . . Look on me and answer, LORD my God," the words capture the pain and uncertainty many of us have felt as we walked through the dark valleys of life. These verses, thousands of years old, articulate the misery in our hearts as if they were composed yesterday. And then, a few verses later, when we read, "But I trust in your unfailing love; . . . I will sing the LORD's, praises for he has been good to me," we see that even in the midst of deep suffering, it is possible for our hope to be renewed.

We can beat on God's chest and wail if we need to. He is big enough to take it. Studying the Bible has helped me learn this essential lesson. It has also helped me learn that God knows more than I do when it comes to how I should live my life. God has a plan for my family, my work, my relationships with other people, and even for my money, that I wouldn't know if I hadn't taken time to read His words in the Bible.

When we open God's Word and give it time to seep into us, to soak our minds completely, we are recapturing Sabbath. We are experiencing a part of the holy rhythm that disciplines us to stay in step with what God is doing in our lives.

Recalibration Is Not Legalism in Disguise

It's important to repeat that the spiritual disciplines we've been discussing are not a way to earn God's favor. They have nothing in common with the headlines you often see on the covers of magazines in the grocery store checkout line: "Five Easy Steps to More Happiness," "Ten Things You Need to Know to Raise Confident Kids," "Three Tips for Saying Goodbye to Belly Fat." But we really crave those step-by-step plans, don't we? It starts in school, with questions like "Is this going to be on the test?" We want to know the requirements we need to check off to get where we want to go or to do what we want to do.

But spiritual disciplines aren't like that. Performing them in an effort to get God to love you more accomplishes nothing. God already loves you more than you could possibly imagine, and there is nothing you can do or not do that is going to change that.

Now, don't get me wrong: I'm not anti-spiritual activity. But I am opposed to spiritual activity that seeks to earn from God the love He has already given so freely.

As Annie Dillard notes in the opening quote, practicing the spiritual disciplines is a way to recalibrate, to see more clearly. It helps us remain connected to the true source of life.

When we aren't seeing them as some sort of religious merit badge, we sometimes tend to think of spiritual disciplines as obligations—chores we must do in order to remain in good standing with God. However, if we see them for what they really are, we would realize that they are actually opportunities. Prayer, Scripture, and contemplation are our invitation to the sacred dance. They attune us to the holy rhythm that binds together God's great, unfolding symphony.

Our problem is that we cannot see as God sees. We see only our impatience with the process or the distractions of our day-to-day lives. But God sees not only where we are now but where we are destined to be and what we are destined to become. And He has given us these disciplines as a way to prepare ourselves.

I heard about an anti-smoking campaign in a Boys and Girls Club where they tried to discourage kids from taking up the habit by telling them smoking would discolor their teeth and would make them smell bad. Apparently, this approach worked with some of the youngsters. Who wants to stink or have ugly teeth?

Of course, the real reason not to smoke is because it can kill you! But the kids at the Boys and Girls Club had trouble looking that far down the road. Because it was next to impossible for them to imagine themselves old enough to have to worry about things like emphysema and lung cancer, the counselors focused on the short-term benefits of staying away from cigarettes.

As far as the spiritual disciplines are concerned, we are a lot like those kids. Even when we grudgingly attempt to incorporate more prayer time into our day or to set aside a half hour for Bible reading, we are more apt to be looking for the short-term payoff, rather than the long-term transformation.

It's kind of interesting to me that we tend to view spiritual formation and the spiritual disciplines the way we do. After all, we admire athletes who keep to a rigorous training schedule, and we don't think they're trying to show off or win points with the coach. We realize they truly want to improve their abilities so they can continue to be successful, but when we think about applying ourselves to spiritual "training," we see it as either drudgery to be avoided as long as possible or as something that qualifies us for bonus points with God.

Perhaps one reason we have trouble viewing the opportunity of spiritual disciplines correctly is that, by their very nature, they require a commitment of time, not just for a few months, but for years. They are, in fact, meant to be a way of life.

Once again, our culture is not geared for something like this. Too often, even in our spiritual lives, we want "microwave spirituality." We want the rush of feeling, the quick, overpowering dose of holiness, so we can move on to the next thing. I am afraid, even in matters of faith, that we are a people who expect instant gratification. But the deep connectedness with God I am talking about just won't happen that way. There are no shortcuts to intimacy with the holy.

We've already talked about the need to commit, not only to God's power and blessing, but to His calendar. It is much the same with acquiring lives of spiritual discipline. They must be built one day at a time, one prayer at a time, one surrender at a time.

And this leads to another obstacle presented by modern society: this type of day-by-day, precept-upon-precept discipline is just not interesting to us. With the power and reach of modern marketing—and especially with the flood of information available to us on the Internet—we are becoming a population with shorter and shorter attention spans. The banner ads, the popups, the clever commercials, the Tweets and follow-backs all teach us that we need to be watching for something new, something exciting, something that is trending now. But in order to walk in step with the Spirit, we must consciously turn away from all that, at least from time to time. We must proactively seek out stretches of quiet and allow our souls to lengthen into the more deliberate rhythm of the sacred.

Eventually, as we practice living with holy rhythm, the steps of the dance start to become part of us. We find that we are spending less time worrying about "doing it right" and more time enjoying the dance for its own sake. We are becoming recalibrated.

How Do You Know when You Need Recalibration?

There are some clues that can tell you when you are due for a spiritual realignment. Of course, it's better if you set aside regular, recurring times to recapture the Sabbath rhythm, but there are also several things you can look for that tell you a spiritual recalibration is overdue.

When your pace of life is too fast for too long, it's time to pull back and recalibrate. We are just not wired to go full-bore, day after day. Eventually, something is going to go *boink*, and we are in for a system crash.

A few years ago, a social anthropologist made the observation that, based on the archaeological evidence, our hunter-gatherer forebears spent about twenty hours per week in focused efforts to secure the food supply. The rest of the time, they made things with their hands, told stories, sang, danced, created art, and ate meals together.

Today, many of us spend sixty to eighty hours per week securing the "food supply," and we're so exhausted the rest of the time that all we do is vegetate in front of the television or sleep. "And," the anthropologist remarked, "we call this progress."

It makes me sad to realize that some of the people who are busiest burning the candle at both ends are my counterparts in ministry. Because of our deep commitment to advancing the kingdom of God, we too often forget that, in order to nurture others, we must have time to nurture ourselves and to be nurtured. And you need to be nurtured, too. When the tread-mill is spinning too fast, learn to step off.

Another telltale sign of the need for recalibration is when you find yourself utilizing certain behaviors as escape mechanisms from the stresses of your life. If you find yourself drinking or using other substances to avoid thinking about what's going on at work or at home, you are trying to avoid your life rather than live it. If you feel the need to spend money in order feel better about yourself or to compensate for some other part of your life, you are probably getting out of alignment. Often the classic workaholic personality is really trying to escape from something. Any behavior—even some that others might view as praiseworthy—that you adopt as a way of not facing up to some aspect of your life that needs to be dealt with is an indication that you are in need of spiritual recalibration.

A general lack of contentment is often a sign that your life is misaligned from God's purposes for you. As Ecclesiastes says, "A person can do nothing better than to eat and drink and find satisfaction in their own toil. This too, I see, is from the hand of God" (Ecclesiastes 2:24). God intends for us to find meaning in our work and to enjoy the simple things of life. If you are finding this difficult, you probably need to reclaim the Sabbath in your heart.

And here's another benefit: you'll also find that as contentment increases, hurry decreases. It's interesting that when we discuss the idea of life moving too fast and being too full, we generally go straight to our calendar to see if we can make some changes. This is usually just a temporary fix, and often, life will go back to being out of control within weeks. Why? Because hurry is not a calendar issue—it's a heart issue. Slowing down starts with your heart, not your planner. If you don't learn to be content in your heart, you'll always return to a hurried life.

But there is good news, as Paul reminds us in Philippians 4:11: "I have learned to be content whatever the circumstances." I think the key word there is "learned." You are not by nature a contented person—and neither am I. It is our nature to want things to be different, to want them to be better, to want them to be something other than they are.

If you find yourself more easily angered than usual or if your reactions to events are starting to seem out of proportion to the actual situation—to yourself or to other people who are significant in your life—it is likely that you need to set aside some time for recalibration.

Really, the common denominator of all these indicators is that each of them, in some way, is an attempt to put ourselves at the center, in control, calling the shots. This goes back to something we discussed at the beginning of the chapter: your life is calibrated with God only when you recognize that God—not you—is the center of everything. Only by committing yourself, over and over, to placing your supreme trust in God and in him only will you remain in sync with the way God means for you to live your life.

It is a simple but profound fact: if you are living in a way that is out of tune with God, you will not have the confidence you need to live out His dreams for your life. Embrace the holy rhythms of the Spirit and the times of Sabbath. God has built a need for these into every human soul. It's the way you were meant to live.

 ## Chapter Eight in Review

Key Ideas

1. The Maker of heaven and earth, our Creator, is our standard. Because we are made in His image, our truest identity is found in Him. There is a holy rhythm involved when we are living in concert with God's dream for our lives.

2. As long as you think you are the central character in the story, you are out of calibration. You're playing out of tune.

3. We are not designed to live our lives out of alignment with God. If we don't periodically recalibrate, something, somewhere is going to get out of whack.

4. Success causes more alignment problems than failure.

5. We need to build "Sabbath" into our lives, not because we're trying to impress others with our spirituality or trying to earn brownie points with God, but because this is how we are wired.

Reflection Questions

1. What are the main obstacles you face in trying to reclaim Sabbath as a regular part of your life?

2. List some good things—worthy causes, life goals, commitments—that can cause us to lose sight of spiritual disciplines like focused prayer, Bible study, and solitude.

3. How does accountability to another person help us reclaim Sabbath practices in our lives?

4. Do you think you measure your self-worth more by what you have accomplished or by what God is doing in you? If your answer is the former, what could you do to rebalance in favor of the latter?

Your Next Step

Set aside one day during the work week when you can spend your lunch hour by yourself in solitude. Instead of going to a restaurant or to the office break room, take a walk outside, or simply close your office door and spend the time in quiet contemplation of a Scripture passage or in prayer. Try to still your mind and make room in your awareness for the vast peace of God.

NINE

LEAN INTO TRANSITION

"You miss 100 percent of the shots you don't take."
—Wayne Gretzky

Marisol was only three years old when her family immigrated to the US from Mexico. Like so many seekers before them, her parents were determined to make a better life for their children than they believed they could provide in their home country. And so, with baby Marisol and all their earthly belongings, they came to this country.

Knowing that education was the most vital key to a better life for their daughter, they enrolled Marisol in the public school of the community where they settled. Because only Spanish was spoken in her home, Marisol received special instruction offered to children learning English as a second language (ESL). It was hard at first, but the little girl loved school, and she persisted.

Marisol proved to be a dedicated student, and she not only completed high school but also was accepted into college. As far as Marisol was concerned, there was only one career worth pursuing: she wanted to be a teacher. Marisol longed to be able to do for other children what the teachers in her life had done for her. (Marisol isn't her real name, but her story is completely true.)

While taking the final courses to prepare her for student teaching, Marisol was fortunate enough to enroll in an education methods class taught by Dr. Janet Hames (not the professor's real name). It so happened that Dr. Hames also sponsored the study-abroad program for the education department at Marisol's college, and Marisol became intrigued by the idea of going to a foreign country. It would be a first for anyone in her family to cross the ocean and visit a different land.

In fact, as the only person in her family to enter college, Marisol was becoming interested in collecting as many "firsts" as she could. When she graduated, she would be the first in her family to achieve a university degree. If she succeeded in obtaining a teaching job, she would be the first in her family to establish a professional career. The problem was that Marisol was deathly afraid of flying. The thought of entering an aircraft and feeling it leave the ground made her break out in a cold sweat.

Nevertheless, the idea of going to another country to study with the charismatic and gifted Dr. Hames just wouldn't turn loose of Marisol's mind. Shyly, she approached her professor about the possibility of scholarships for the study-abroad course. After all, her family needed all the assistance they could scrape together just to keep her in school. There was no way they'd be able to come up with the extra several thousand dollars required to pay for the study-abroad course. Wisely, Dr. Hames assured Marisol that scholarships and other assistance for the trip were certainly available, and she aided Marisol with completing applications and writing for grants. Marisol's trip costs would be covered.

But that didn't take care of her fear of flying. As the departure date drew nearer, Marisol was tortured by nightmares featuring Technicolor disaster scenarios: airplanes falling from the sky, terrified screams, cabins filled with smoke, the horrified realization that she would never see her parents again. Still, Marisol hung in there. This "first" had become very important to her. Something deep within her whispered that this course, this trip could change her life in a way she didn't expect.

Afraid of becoming nauseated on the flight, Marisol took motion sickness pills. To her surprise and relief, the pills also helped her relax enough to go to sleep, and when she awoke, the aircraft was on the ground in Spain.

For the next six weeks, Marisol was in an almost perpetual state of delight. She was fascinated by aspects of the unfamiliar Spanish culture. She was very interested in the many differences between the way Mexicans spoke Spanish and the way European speakers communicated. She soaked in the majesty of Barcelona's Sagrada Familia Cathedral. She explored the world-renowned Prado National Art Museum in Madrid, and she poured herself into the coursework, which included significant interaction with classes of Spanish schoolchildren who were studying English—an ironic reversal of her own earliest schooling experiences.

By the end of the course, Marisol realized she almost didn't want to leave. Travel had become her new passion. On the way home, instead of taking motion sickness pills, she watched movies.

After her return to the US, Marisol finished her education degree and received her teaching certification. She also realized there was a way to combine her original passion—teaching—with her newfound passion for travel. Marisol decided to teach outside the borders of the US. Today, she is a successful educator in a Central American country. When her duties permit, she travels widely, eager to learn as much as she can about the people and the culture in and around her newfound home.

When Your Fear Is Camouflaging Your Passion

I am convinced that fear defeats more dreams than all other causes combined. Like Marisol, many of us find fear standing between us and the pursuit of our passion. Unlike Marisol, however, many of us surrender to the fear and resign ourselves to a life that is so much less than it could be.

But what if we could learn to lean into the fear, into the transition? What if we could take the first step toward pursuit of the dream, and then the next, and the one after that?

Certainly, doing that requires going forward in the face of uncertainty. As we've already discussed, none of us ever gets 100 percent clarity about the finish line while we're standing at the starting gate. Only by moving forward are we able to begin to see what might be next.

Without a doubt, leaning into transition requires much of us. It will mean encountering stress, uncertainty, cost, discomfort, and a certain amount of temporary chaos. It will require us to learn new skills and acquire new relationships. None of these processes is without risk.

Leaning into transition may even require a certain amount of faking it until you make it. You may need to learn some improvisation skills. After all, you are taking steps into the unknown, the untried. You're going off-script. You may have to wing it for a while.

In Matthew 14, the Bible records the story of Jesus walking on the water. Just before this takes place, He had performed a great miracle, feeding five thousand people with only a little boy's five loaves of bread and two fish as His starting point. After that, He sent His disciples in a boat across the Sea of Galilee while He went away from everyone to spend most of the night in prayer.

Just before dawn the next morning, He went out to the boat, walking across the water. The disciples weren't making much headway in their craft because there was a strong headwind. As they saw Jesus approaching, they were frightened at first—which kind of makes sense, right? I mean, seeing someone walking across the water toward you isn't the sort of thing you normally expect. But Jesus called to them and told them not to be afraid. "It is I," He said.

Peter—possibly the owner of the boat since he was a fisherman by trade—called out, "Lord, if it is really You, let me walk on the water to You."

Jesus told him to come ahead, and Peter started climbing out of the boat.

Hit the "pause" button for a second. Imagine for a moment that you are Peter. As a fisherman—and, likely, the son of a fisherman—you have spent the vast majority of your life on and near the Sea of Galilee. At no time during those thousands of hours in, on, and around the water, have you ever seen water support the weight of a person so that it could be walked on. You have never even heard a story about a time when such a thing happened. Remember, we aren't in the Arctic Circle here. This is liquid, flowing water—and you are climbing out of your boat, getting ready to plant your feet on it as if it is solid ground.

Why would Peter do something like this—something that makes absolutely no sense, based on a lifetime of experience? I think it is because of the desire burning in Peter's heart: to be near Jesus. At that moment, the thing he wanted most in all the world was to stand next to his teacher, atop the waves.

So, Peter clambers out of the boat and takes off, headed toward Jesus, but then something happens: fear gets in the way. The Bible says Peter "saw the wind" and was afraid—and he began to sink. Peter realized he was completely off-script. He was in a situation that no previous experience of his life had prepared him for. He was on uncharted ground—oops, I mean uncharted water. And he became afraid.

Fortunately for Peter, he was in the vicinity of the only Person in the world ever known to have walked on water. Jesus grabbed Peter's hand and helped him back into the boat.

We can talk about Peter's lapse in faith, of course. We can discuss how his fear got in the way of the pursuit of his goal, but we have to give him credit for getting out of the boat, don't we? And from Peter's experience, we can also learn that leaning into transition in the pursuit of a dream will often put us in situations we never expected. In fact, the unexpected seems to be part and parcel of taking those first steps.

So, the first fear we often have to face is our fear of the unexpected. And it's in the midst of that fear that we have to find the courage to accept every experience—including the negative ones—as merely steps on the path. And then we have to proceed.

Commit to the Long Haul

One thing you have to say for Peter is that, even if it was fleeting, he was willing to put his faith into action. He took the step. In fact, the type of faith Jesus speaks of most frequently is characterized by action—stepping out of the boat in belief, even when you've never seen somebody walk on water before.

But unlike Peter's experience in this case, the faith to lean into transition also requires a commitment to stay the course, no matter how long it takes. It is marathon faith, not sprint faith. It is the type of belief that will not turn back at the first obstacle, or the second, or the third. Instead, with its confidence placed in God, rather than circumstances, it will persevere.

This is not merely the power of positive thinking. Leaning into transition goes far beyond forced optimism or the latest pop psychology self-talk. It arises out of a sense of urgency for the realization of the dream. It is driven by the utter belief in God's purpose for our lives, and it is bolstered by the preparation we have made in order to participate meaningfully in that purpose.

We must also be committed to and engaged in the process. We are not floating wistfully along, idly hoping that the winds blow us in the direction we wish to go. Instead, we are actively participating. Like Peter, we are stepping out of the boat on the Lord's say-so. We are doing the next right thing, depending on God to help us see what follows from that.

There is perhaps no better image of hoping for the best and planning for the worst than soldiers preparing to go into battle. What could possibly be more uncertain than war? Where could anybody encounter more risk, more stress, more anxiety? And yet, the soldiers have taken a solemn oath to defend their homeland. They have sworn to obey their leaders, even in the face of a hostile enemy. The desire for a victory that leads to peace propels them to prepare tirelessly, to learn everything possible about their own tactics and the enemy's, to hone their abilities in preparation for the coming conflict. The solders are fully engaged, participating wholeheartedly in bringing about the hoped-for outcome, even though they know that great difficulty and extreme uncertainty lie ahead. They are committed for the long haul.

Fueling the Fire Within

Many people are motivated to move past their fears and in the direction of their passion by activating what Bill Hybels calls "holy discontent." In his book by the same title, Hybels explains that, when we consider the problems in our world, that particular situation we "just can't stand" and that we cannot get out of our minds is usually the locus of our holy discontent—a passion sent from God and ignited by our particular response to some aspect of the world's need.

For example, I know of two college students in Texas who became convicted about the problem of sex trafficking. The horror of young girls being abducted and victimized as they were sent into the maw of the sex trade was an image these two young women simply could not get out of their minds. So, they decided to take action. They founded a group called the Red Thread Movement that sponsored efforts to rescue women and girls from the sex trade, with a concentration in the nation of Nepal, where sex trafficking is a major industry. Every year, an estimated eleven thousand women and girls are trafficked from Nepal into India and other destinations. They are sold into the sex trade by their families, by their husbands, and by kidnappers.

The Red Thread Movement got its name from the simple red thread bracelets—woven by the rescued women—that the movement sells to raise money for funding its efforts. The money goes to pay a fair wage to women who make the bracelets and also to fund efforts of the border monitors and halfway houses that form the all-important first links in the chain of the rescue effort. The border monitors are women who stand at border crossings all day, watching for women who exhibit the signs of trafficking victims. Once they are identified and taken away from traffickers, the rescued women are taken to one of three safe houses operated by the Red Thread Movement's partner organization in Nepal. There, the women receive training, counseling and, most important of all, hope.

None of this would be possible without the efforts of these two visionary and passionate young women who paid attention to their holy discontent. They found the place in their hearts, described by Frederick Buechner, where their passion intersected with the world's deep need. And they had the courage to follow where that passion led. At last count, this grassroots organization, started by two college students, was helping to fund the rescue of some fifteen hundred victims per year.

What fuels your inner fire? It may well be that the thing keeping you up at night is not fear but passion. I urge you to listen to that passion. It may very well be the dream God has shaped for you to fulfill.

Something interesting happens to those who begin following their passion: fear is replaced by a sense of calling. They become more focused on the object of their passion than they formerly were on the fear that was blocking the path.

The process reminds me of a vivid scene in C. S. Lewis's allegorical tale *The Great Divorce*. Portraying various souls in the process of trying to enter heaven, Lewis describes the temptations and obstacles they must face and overcome—or, in some tragic cases, are defeated by. One of these is a young man who has a lizard-like thing clamped to his shoulder. Through Lewis's deft description, we come to understand that the lizard represents lust and that this parasitic being constantly whispers its lewd suggestions and observations into the young man's ear.

Sadly, the young man cannot imagine what his life would be like without the lizard. He sees it as a part of himself. But as long as he allows the lizard to cling to his shoulder, he cannot enter the heavenly country.

An angel approaches the young man and asks if he wants to be delivered of his whispering passenger. The young man deeply desires to enter heaven, but at the same time, he cannot bear to think of existence apart from the lizard. In fact, he thinks that if he is separated from its attentions, he will die.

Finally, in desperation, the young man cries, "God help me!"

That is all the invitation the angel needs. He grasps the lizard and tears it, screaming, from the young man's shoulder. The lizard falls writhing to the ground, but, instead of dying, it is transformed into a beautiful, spirited horse.

The young man, enthralled, mounts upon the horse and, with the angel's blessing, gallops off toward the hills of heaven. We realize that his lust—a weak, parasitic emotion—was transformed by the angel into the inspired passion that could propel him on to become all that he was created to be.

Much the same thing happens when we find the courage to follow the passions God places in our hearts. When we follow our passion and allow it to be channeled into action, we realize that our former fears are not as formidable as we first thought. Instead, the uncertainties and worries that seemed so insurmountable before have receded. Propelled by divine discontent, we notice less and less our impediments and problems, while noticing more and more the opportunities lying before us and the tools God is giving us to take advantage of them. We receive the strength that comes with conviction and the vision that comes with faith. And while this does not mean that all difficulties will disappear, it does mean that we are much better equipped to handle them than we were when we were standing still, mired in fear of the unknown.

But we must take the first steps in faith. Like Peter, we have to be willing to climb out of the boat, out of the familiar patterns of life as we have always known it. And once we take that first step on the waves, we have to keep our eyes fixed on Jesus. If we start watching the wind, as Peter did, fear steps in once again, and we may find ourselves trapped and in need of rescue.

We have to remember that the life Jesus calls us to is one of motion. The way we describe this at Cross Point is to "Go and Love." The gospel does not call just for reflection, but for action. We are always traveling toward higher ground, following what Paul refers to as the "high calling of God in Christ Jesus" (Philippians 3:14 KJV).

When You Can't Sit Still

So, as you think about your purpose, pay close attention to those images and visions you just can't get out of your head. Do you see a problem that needs to be fixed? Do you see an injustice that must be addressed? Do you see marginalized people that someone needs to reach out to? Do you see a better way, a more fitting solution, a fairer method, a quicker path?

These visions, desires, and enthusiasms may very well be where God is shaping your passion to meet the world's deep need. Follow where they lead you. If you need more knowledge, find out where you can get it. If you need advice, look for someone who can give it to you. If you need resources, start taking steps to secure them. The point is, you will never become any more qualified to begin the journey than you are right now.

So, begin! Clarity only comes when you are in motion, and perfect clarity, as we learned from the story of Joseph, only comes with hindsight. Let your passion guide your resolve. Act on it. Move ahead. If God is calling you to accomplish it, you can rest in the assurance that He will equip you with what you need to get it done. Prepare for the long haul. Commit yourself to staying in the game long enough to see God transform your fears into your deep passion.

Staying in the Game

One of my favorite people in the Bible is David. He is called "a man after God's own heart," but it isn't because he was perfect—far from it.

While it is true that David had a passion for God matched by few others in the history of the world, it is also true that he made many poor decisions. He also endured one of the longest and most arduous waits on record on the road to seeing his desires come to fruition.

David was anointed to be the next king of Israel when he was still a boy, living at the home of his father, Jesse. In fact, at the time of his anointing, David was the youngest of seven boys. He was the kid brother, stuck out in the pasture with the sheep.

But God didn't look at David the same way everyone else did. He told His prophet Samuel, "The LORD does not look at the things people look at. People look at the outward appearance, but the LORD looks at the heart" (1 Samuel 16:7). And Samuel anointed David to be the next king of Israel.

The problem was that there was still someone on the throne, and his name was Saul. Though Saul, through his disobedience was not pleasing to God, he would continue to be the king of Israel for another fifteen years. During that time, David would go from nobody to superstar status—after killing the giant Philistine warrior, Goliath, and accomplishing many other feats of prowess in Saul's service—and then to being a fugitive with a price on his head.

Saul became jealous of David's success and his growing popularity, and he even tried to kill him with a spear as David sat singing and playing his harp to soothe Saul's foul temper. David spent years on the run, gradually gathering to himself a band of fighters—sort of like Robin Hood and his merry men. He had to be constantly on the watch for Saul, who seemed to grow to hate him more and more as time passed.

Remember that while all this is going on, David knows he has been anointed as God's chosen king! Do you think he ever questioned all the problems he was having? Do you think he ever got discouraged and wondered if maybe he had just imagined that whole scene with the old dude pouring oil on his head and saying he would be king someday?

I'm not sure what he thought about all this, but I do know that David never lost the desire that God had placed in his heart. He wrote scores of psalms—the most beautiful poetry in the Bible—recording his longing for God and his confidence in the Lord's ultimate deliverance.

And remarkably, David never sought vengeance on Saul. Even though Saul had lost God's blessing, David still regarded him as the Lord's anointed. Once, David could have killed Saul himself, but instead, he silently sliced off a piece of Saul's robe and later displayed it in front of Saul, to show that the king had nothing to fear from David.

Throughout all his fifteen years as a hunted man, David continued to believe. He continued to prepare himself for the day when he would receive the crown and throne God had promised him. He followed God's lead wherever it took him, and when he messed up, no one ever repented as completely as David did.

All during the time of his career—first as a champion in Saul's cause and then as an outlaw on the run—God was preparing David for the day when his path to the throne would be clear. As he fought Saul's enemies (sometimes even when Saul was trying to hunt him down), as he led his band of fighters about the country, and as he dealt with the various types of people he encountered in his journeys, all the time David was learning what he would need to know to rule Israel effectively. And the day came, just as God had promised, when Saul was no more, and David was fully prepared to assume the role he had been promised since the day Samuel had come to his father's house and anointed him. At the age of thirty, David—Jesse's baby boy—sat down on the throne of Israel.

David held the desire in his heart. He prepared himself for it to become a reality. He kept on doing the next right thing. He committed himself to the long haul, and he saw the promise come to pass, just as God had said it would.

Like David, you may face a long and complicated time of uncertainty before you see your passion bear fruit. You may spend a lot of time wandering in your own "desert" of obstacles, opposition, and unexpected difficulties. But if you commit to the long haul and lean into the transition, trusting in God to equip you for whatever you need to do, you will one day see your purposes fulfilled and your fears conquered. It may not take the shape you imagined for it in the beginning, but it will be perfect, as with all things God designs.

Chapter Nine in Review

Key Ideas

1. Many of us find fear standing between us and the pursuit of our passion.
2. Leaning into transition may require a certain amount of faking it until you make it.
3. The type of faith Jesus speaks of most frequently is characterized by action.
4. It may well be that the thing keeping you up at night is not fear but passion.
5. If God is calling you to accomplish it, you can rest in the assurance that He will equip you with what you need to get it done.

Reflection Questions

1. What would you attempt right now, if you knew it was impossible for you to fail?
2. Think of a time when you "stepped out of the boat," only to start sinking. Looking back on that experience, if you could give yourself one piece of advice, what would it be?
3. How do you think David was able to keep going for fifteen years, knowing he was meant to be king, yet still seeing Saul on the throne? What do you think kept him from giving up?

Your Next Step

Make a list of everything going on the world that fuels your passion or provokes your "holy discontent." Commit to placing these things before God in prayer each day for a month. See what happens.

TEN

LIVE FOR THE ADVENTURE

"Safe?" said Mr. Beaver.... "Who said
anything about safe? 'Course he isn't safe.
But he's good. He's the King, I tell you."
—C. S. Lewis

A few years ago, New Line Cinema released *Pleasantville*, described as a "modern fairy tale" in which two teens, played by Tobey Maguire and Reese Witherspoon, find themselves inexplicably transported into a 1950s sitcom set in a place called Pleasantville: a black-and-white world where everything happens the way it's supposed to. When the varsity basketball players take a shot, it always goes in. Dad comes home from work the same time every day, and Mom always has his newspaper waiting and his dinner on the stove.

In Pleasantville there is no crime, no cheating, no

delinquency—juvenile or otherwise. There is also no color, no great art, and no passion. Everything is predictable and safe.

You can probably see where the conflict comes into this story. None of us can imagine living in a world where all outcomes are known. All of us yearn, at some level, for the thrill and challenge of something new and unexpected—even if it comes with the price tag of a certain amount of danger.

Why else would people do things like rock climbing or whitewater rafting? Why would anyone voluntarily jump out of a perfectly good airplane with a parachute strapped to her back?

Something within us instinctively craves the adventure, the testing of the uncontrollable future. There's a tiny bit of hero in each of us. We long to test our mettle against the unforeseen trial. We want the chance to overcome, to prove ourselves.

This isn't limited to superheroes or outdoor types. I know of a young actor who, for a time, traveled with a professional touring company. He told me that after a long enough time on the road, performing the same shows day in and day out, he and his fellow actors used to secretly hope for something to go wrong during a show—a dropped sound cue, a blown line, a missing prop, anything to force them out of the rut of the familiar and the predictable. They craved the adventure and the challenge of dealing with the unexpected in front of a live audience.

Jesus Never Promised Safety

The life spent in pursuit of God's purposes and plans is not a life of security and safety. When Jesus says, in John 10:10, "I am come that they might have life, and that they might have it more abundantly" (KJV), He is not offering us a safety net. Instead, He is calling us to life on the edge, to the kind of life that is pursued with passion, chasing a dream.

As a matter of fact, of all the many promises Jesus gives us, safety is not anywhere to be found. He promises us trouble in this world (John 16:33) but immediately asserts that He is mightier than this world. He assures us that we will be falsely accused and spoken ill of (Matthew 5:11), but He also tells us that we will receive the same reward in heaven as God's faithful prophets who were similarly abused. He warns us that the world may hate us (John 15:18) but reminds us that it hated Him first.

And when you think about it, how could it be any other way? Try to come up with a single great thing in the history of mankind that was accomplished entirely without risk. I'll save you some time—you can't.

Even God is not immune from risk. When He created human beings in His own image and gave them free will, He risked losing their affection and obedience. But He was willing to take that chance because He wanted children who could love Him back of their own accord, not automatons who only did what they were programmed to do.

The life lived in pursuit of a deeply desired goal is characterized by a relentless pace. We are drawn on by the urgency of the goal; we cannot truly rest until our driving passion is realized. We are propelled by an inner hunger that is greater than our fears. And when our passion is coupled with God's unfolding destiny, we are sustained by His strength. Our emerging needs are supplied from His inexhaustible bounty.

Corrie ten Boom, the courageous saint who endured the horrors of Ravensbruck because of her efforts to protect Jews during World War II, relates in her memoir, *Tramp for the Lord*, the words shared with her by her sister Betsie, just before Betsie died in the camp:

> "Corrie, there is so much bitterness. We must tell them that the Holy Spirit will fill their hearts with God's love. . . . we will travel the world bringing the gospel to all—our friends as well as our enemies."
>
> Corrie said, "To all the world? But that will take much money."
>
> Betsie replied, "Yes, but God will provide. We must do nothing else but bring the gospel, and He will take care of us. After all, He owns the cattle on a thousand hills. If we need money, we will just ask the Father to sell a few cows."[1]

That is the type of faith that overcomes fear—faith that realizes no matter what challenges may lie in front of us, we always have behind us a God who is greater than any challenge.

A Hunger for Tomorrow

The stories we tell over and over again are all tales rich with adventure. The books we remember are those that draw us on, from page to page, eager to see what happens next.

Sam Gamgee knew this very well, didn't he? As he and

his beloved master Frodo are trudging toward greater danger than they know in their quest to reach Mordor and destroy the evil One Ring, he says to Frodo:

> We shouldn't be here at all, if we'd known more about it before we started. But I suppose it's often that way. The brave things in the old tales and songs, Mr. Frodo: adventures, as I used to call them. . . . Folk seem to have been just landed in them, usually—their paths were laid that way. . . . But I expect they had lots of chances, like us, of turning back, only they didn't. And if they had, we shouldn't know, because they'd have been forgotten.[2]

Sam is right, isn't he? The stories we most love to tell and to hear are about the characters who kept on in the face of uncertainty—before they knew how things would turn out. We best remember the ones who didn't turn back.

In the same way, when we are following our passion, we long to see what's coming next in our lives. We are eager for the next episode—be it happy or sad, easy or hard—because we know the only way is forward, through whatever is about to happen.

Fear tries to convince us that our present reality is all there is—that the future only holds more of the same, into infinity. But faith tells us the truth: that God has things in store for us that we could never have imagined for ourselves. Or, as Paul phrases it, "Eye hath not seen, nor ear heard, neither have entered into the heart of man, the things which God hath prepared for them that love him" (1 Corinthians 2:9 KJV).

When we live by faith, we press forward, eager to see the unfolding of God's unimaginable blessings. The hope we carry is refreshed and resupplied, even amid harsh trial, when we step out in the direction of God's dreams for us.

The Spirit Within

Remember: you are made in God's image. Just as He did with Adam, He has breathed into you the breath of life. You have become a living soul.

In Hebrew, the word for "breath"—*ruach*—is also the word for "spirit." So, when we say that God's breath is in you, we are also saying that His Spirit is in you.

The Latin word for "soul" is *anima*. When something is living and active, we say it is "animated." It has life within it. It has spirit.

Sit for a moment with that truth. The Spirit of God—His life, His animating force—is *in you*. Every movement you make, every thought that goes through your mind, is empowered by the Spirit of the living God. You have a life force within you that longs to imitate its Creator. The Spirit of God wants to create, to renew, to bring into being that which is not presently seen.

And God longs to see you accomplish this. It is not His wish to see any of His beloved children living lives of dull predictability or mere safety. The spark He has placed within you is meant to kindle a fire. It is meant to propel you out into the world, seeking the places where your particular passion is required to bring healing, hope, and comfort where before there was only discouragement, injustice, and wrong.

Think about it this way: nobody ever built a boat in order to have it sit safely on its blocks and be admired for the cleverness of its construction. A boat is made to be out on the water, washed by the waves and even, sometimes, battered by strong winds and storm spray. Boats are made for going places, for taking people somewhere they would otherwise be unable to go.

The Hero Within

Back in 1984, Bonnie Tyler sang what many people were thinking when her hit song "Holding Out for a Hero" was blasting from radios across the country. Most of us, at various times in our lives, can resonate with her assertion in the chorus: "I need a hero!"

In fact, in every corner of the world, through every moment in history, and even before history, people have always needed a hero. In his monumental and influential books *The Hero with a Thousand Faces* and *The Hero's Journey*, Joseph Campbell helps us understand that in all human cultures, stories of heroes bear similar traits. As it turns out, we not only need our heroes, we need them to do very particular things.

One of the most basic beginnings of every hero story—be it Chinese, Indian, African, German, Irish, or Native American— is when the hero receives the call into adventure. At this point, according to Campbell, the hero leaves behind the ordinary world that is all most mortals will ever know and enters the world of enchantment and wonder—the place where adventures and dangerous trials await.

The call to adventure can happen in many different ways, and you can see this by merely recollecting a few of the stories we all love most:

- For Alice, the call to adventure comes from noticing a white rabbit scurrying past—but this rabbit is peering at a pocket watch and wearing a vest.
- Huckleberry Finn took it upon himself to grab a raft and float down the Mississippi River in a quest to save his friend Jim from a lifetime of slavery.
- For Dorothy, the summons came by means of a tornado that transported her bodily into the adventure world.
- Bilbo Baggins is summoned to adventure by Gandalf.
- Jack encounters adventure when he trades his family's cow for a handful of magic beans.

But the real question is this: How will *your* adventure begin?

It may be that you notice, one day, nobody is taking enough notice of the homeless family, living in their car, to help them get their basic needs met. When you decide to find out what you can do about it, you take your first step beyond the boundary of the "normal" world.

Or it could be that you will finally decide to send to a magazine editor that article you've been tinkering with for two years. You climb on your charger, take up your lance, and ride off to face the fearsome dragon named Rejection.

Maybe you will one day get so fed up with the shoddy way your company deals with its customers that you will act on your desire to start your own business, dedicated to doing it right the first time, no matter what it takes. You decide to strike a blow at the ogre named Mediocrity.

You might decide that you are tired of watching your marriage die, a little at a time. You push past your fear that nothing is going to change, and you pick up the phone to dial the number of a counselor. You are leaving behind the world where everything stays the same and entering the land of possibility.

You may come to the point where you can no longer tolerate the way your community treats people on the margins of society. You speak up, you step out, and you start to organize. You cross the frontier that separates "the way it's always been" from the way you think it ought to be.

For me, it happened five years ago, when I took my first trip to India. I made some cherished friends on that trip and saw things I never imagined seeing, but I'll never forget the moment when God put it on my heart that my life would be forever connected with the people of Kolkata, India.

We were touring a slum just outside of the city when our tour guide just mentioned in passing that there was no church, nor had there ever been a church in this slum. The nonprofit organization I was traveling with only works through local churches, which meant they were not able to establish a project in this slum, either.

I immediately had this thought: *Pete, you can help. You can help start a church in this slum.* It took a few years to get things up and running, but that initial thought led to a nonprofit called One Life that has helped plant several churches, build schools, and feed hundreds of kids each day around Kolkata, India.

Were there challenges in getting those churches planted? Oh, yeah. Were there moments when I was terrified that the effort would fail in a very public and embarrassing way? Sure. Did we have to overcome financial, bureaucratic, spiritual, and emotional obstacles in order to see our plans come to fruition? We sure did—in spades. But by the grace and provision of God, ministry in his name is now happening in that slum and in others in India. What an adventure!

I don't know what is going on in your life or your heart. I'm not sure what particular fears or demons are keeping you in place, preventing you from crossing over from the world of the same-old-same-old to the scary, exhilarating, challenging, dangerous realm of the hero's journey. But I guarantee you this: there is a quest out there with your name on it. And I'll lay odds on one more thing: you already know what it is.

Through the Valley

Every hero, at some point in the journey, faces a dark passage, an ultimate trial. In fact, you could even say that this is what defines a hero.

Joseph Campbell characterizes this aspect of the hero's journey as "the descent into the abyss" or being "in the belly of the whale." It is here, Campbell says, that the hero faces the most fundamental challenge, and it is also here, upon meeting the challenge, that the hero is reborn.

It isn't too difficult to see the implications of this for followers of Jesus Christ. As the ultimate Hero, Jesus faced humanity's final and most intractable opponent—death—and emerged victorious. It was a harrowing experience, and it required of Jesus the most unwavering faith and the most undaunted courage the world has ever seen. But face the challenge He did—and He beat it!

For us, this means we cannot tread any path that our Hero has not already trod before us. There is no demon, no monster, no enemy we can ever face on our journey—including death—that our Hero has not already conquered. No matter what your quest is or where it takes you, Jesus Christ has already been there before you to show you the way.

If you choose to step across the border from the "normal" world into the life of adventure, you will face trials, obstacles, and maybe even hostile, active opposition. These are part and parcel of the hero's journey. There can be no adventure without the possibility of danger, difficulty, and even failure. But because of Jesus, we can also see the possibility of success, victory, and transformation. The story of our Hero tells us that though there may be a cross in our future, there is also a resurrection waiting on the other side.

I love the story Max Lucado tells in his first book, *On*

the Anvil. He recalls a time when he was a boy, growing up in Andrews, Texas, and he, his brother, and some other boys decided to dig a tunnel in a vacant lot. It was summer, and they didn't have anything else to do, so they managed to dig a trench three feet wide and four feet deep that ran half the length of the lot.

They covered the top of the trench with scraps of plywood, and then they camouflaged it with dirt. They hid the entrance and exit with some brush. It was the perfect underground hideout for a bunch of energetic boys. But someone had to test the tunnel.

Lucado tells how his older brother volunteered. Everybody watched solemnly as he took a couple of deep breaths, then squatted down and crawled into the darkness. The boys' hearts pounded as they watched the exit. After what seemed like forever, Max's brother poked his head out the other end. He stood, waved, and grinned. The rest of the boys piled in; they now knew there was nothing to fear!

That's the way it is with Jesus, our Hero, and us. He has walked every step of the hero's journey, He has faced the deepest, darkest, most horrible trials, and He has come out victorious on the other side. We don't have to be afraid.

You've Got Company

And here's some more good news: once you begin walking the path of the hero's journey, you realize you're not alone. Many times, you will notice, if you look behind you, that a whole bunch of other people have decided to walk it, too. All they needed was to see you step out in faith, determined not to settle any longer for the world of the same-old-same-old. It turns out that they needed a hero—and it's you!

In most cases, you will never know how God is using you in someone else's life. It may be that the song you write is the one that gives a young girl hope when she was thinking about suicide. It may be that the homeless shelter where you volunteer is the place that helps the single mom survive long enough to kick her meth habit. It may be that the company you start becomes the first employer of the dad who just got out of prison and is trying to put his life back together and reclaim a place in his kids' lives. It may be that your faith and peace in the face of serious illness is what allows someone else to think that God may be for real, after all.

You just don't know what can happen, once you decide to overcome your fears and live for adventure.

 ## Chapter Ten in Review

Key Ideas

1. All of us yearn, at some level, for the thrill and challenge of something new and unexpected—even if it comes with the price tag of a certain amount of danger.
2. Of all the many promises Jesus gives us, safety is not anywhere to be found.

3. When our passion is coupled with God's unfolding destiny, we are sustained by His strength. Our emerging needs are supplied from His inexhaustible bounty.

4. The stories we most love to tell and to hear are about the characters who kept on in the face of uncertainty, before they knew how things would turn out. We best remember the ones who didn't turn back.

5. You have a life force within you that longs to imitate its Creator.

6. There is a quest out there with your name on it.

Reflection Questions

1. Who is your favorite hero, either from story or from history? What do you most admire about him or her?

2. Which do you think are harder to face: External enemies or internal ones? What are the differences between them?

3. Do you think there are times when safety is harmful? How could safety be bad for us?

Your Next Step

Imagine that you have embarked upon your quest. What obstacle do you think you will face first? Write a thorough description of the obstacle, and then write down a plan for dealing with it successfully.

ELEVEN

ANTICIPATE CONFIRMATION

"Twice blessed is help unlooked for, and never
was a meeting of friends so joyful."
—J. R. R. Tolkien

It is difficult to imagine a much more dramatic scene than the one described in Joshua chapter 3. The long-awaited day has finally arrived. The children of Israel, who followed Moses out of Egypt and have been wandering in the desert for forty years, are about to cross the Jordan River and enter the Promised Land. They are about to take possession of the inheritance God promised them so long ago.

But there's a problem: the Jordan River is at flood stage.

Between the Israelites and their promised territory lies a raging, muddy torrent, and they aren't carrying rafts or canoes with them. How can an entire nation—women, children, supplies, and livestock, not to mention warriors with all their gear—possibly hope to get across this natural barrier and still be able to move and fight when they reach the other side? God said to Joshua:

> Today I will begin to exalt you in the eyes of all Israel, so they may know that I am with you as I was with Moses. Tell the priests who carry the ark of the covenant: "When you reach the edge of the Jordan's waters, go and stand in the river." (Joshua 3:7–8)

Joshua then announced to all the people:

> See, the ark of the covenant of the Lord of all the earth will go into the Jordan ahead of you. . . . And as soon as the priests who carry the ark of the LORD—the Lord of all the earth—set foot in the Jordan, its waters flowing downstream will be cut off and stand up in a heap." (Joshua 3:11, 13)

Now, you may be thinking this ought to sound very familiar to the Israelites. After all, didn't God do something similar when He parted the Red Sea to save them from the pursuing Egyptian army, back at the very beginning of the Exodus? Yes, He did. But remember: there are only a handful of people still alive at this point who witnessed that event. Because of the people's unbelief some forty years earlier—when Joshua, Caleb, and the other ten spies had gone in to scope out Canaan—God caused them to wander in the wilderness until the entire unbe-lieving generation had died.

By this time, God's miraculous deliverance at the Red Sea is no more than a story some of the people heard their par-ents or grandparents tell. Nevertheless, the next morning, after they had broken camp, the priests took up the ark of the covenant and started marching toward the muddy, turbulent river—and the people fell in line behind them.

I can imagine the scene unfolding: the huge mass of people, moving steadily toward the river, with the priests and the ark of the covenant in the lead. As the priests step closer and closer, the river continues to tumble past—wide, deep, and threaten-ing. They are ten steps away, and the river still looks the same. Five steps . . . three . . . one.

A Little Help, Please

At this point, the crossing of the Jordan looks a lot like a bad idea, doesn't it? Clearly, Joshua and the Israelites do not have the resources they need to overcome the obstacle to their quest. They don't have the materials for either a bridge or enough boats to float everyone across safely. They are going to need some help, or this adventure is going nowhere.

It's the same with us when we step out of the same-old-same-old and onto the path of ruthlessly trusting God. There will be looming problems and difficulties we may not have anticipated. We will face opposition we didn't know was coming. Doubts, fears, and worries will rise up in our path, but God never calls any of His children to a task without providing for their needs. He is a God of surprises, and time and time again, He delivers help and hope when it is least expected. Sometimes, in fact, I think God invented the phrase "the nick of time."

That's what happened with Joshua and the Israelites at the Jordan River. The Bible says:

> [A]s soon as the priests who carried the ark reached the Jordan and their feet touched the water's edge, the water from upstream stopped flowing. It piled up in a heap a great distance away . . . while the water flowing down to the Sea of the Arabah (that is, the Dead Sea) was completely cut off. So the people crossed over opposite Jericho. The priests who carried the ark of the covenant of the LORD stopped in the middle of the Jordan and stood on dry ground, while all Israel passed by until the whole nation had completed the crossing on dry ground. (Joshua 3:15–17)

Now, what do you think would have happened if the priests, noticing that they were getting pretty close to the water and it looked like nothing was happening, decided to stop moving forward? My guess is that the Jordan would have just kept on rolling. The nation of Israel would have been stranded on the wrong side of destiny.

I believe the lesson in this for us is that when God tells us to move out and watch what He's getting ready to do, we'd better start walking and looking. The great preacher Marshall Keeble used to say, "If God tells me to jump through a brick wall, it's up to me to jump, and it's up to God to make the hole."

That's what Joshua did. He grabbed hold of the desire that God had planted in his heart, and he began moving forward, expecting God to make the hole. He anticipated confirmation of his obedience to the destiny God had planned for him and his people.

Living Free

Did you ever wonder why the generation that Joshua led across the Jordan could do what the generation before them could not? I think a big part of the answer has to do with their ability to believe that God would really do what He promised. And in order to believe that, they had to learn to see themselves differently than the previous generation had.

I read an interesting article the other day about how difficult it is for inmates coming out of prison to adjust to being free citizens again. More than four out of ten adult offenders nationwide return to state prisons within three years of their release, studies show.

I read the story of a man named Randall Church who spent twenty-six years in prison for stabbing and killing another man. After ninety-six days of freedom, he purposely set a house on fire and burned it to the ground and immediately turned himself in so he could be arrested and return to prison.

He literally could not handle his freedom. He could not see himself as able to live successfully "on the outside."

Something like that seems to have happened to the people of Israel. They had lived as slaves for four hundred years then suddenly were released from captivity. They were free, but they didn't know how to live as free people. Generation after generation had lived and died in bondage, so they didn't know any other way.

When God called them to trust Him, they just couldn't muster up the courage to do it. Instead they reverted back to fear. They were free, but they continued living in bondage.

There's a difference between *being* free and *living* free.

Confirmation Through Relationships

God gives us courage for our journey in many ways. One way I think we often receive confirmation is through our relationships—either those we already had or, very often, those we acquire along the path to the dream. In fact, in many of the world's great hero stories, one of the essential stages of the quest is the acquisition of a mentor or helper—a person met along the path of the quest who provides essential aid, advice, wisdom, or equipping.

The original *mentor*, of course, was a person: the wise counselor who offered advice to Odysseus's son during his father's long absence. We learn that Mentor was actually the goddess Athena in disguise. Not only was she helping Odysseus, her favorite, during his perilous journey, but she was also helping his son make good decisions in order to preserve Odysseus's home and resources.

Story and, nowadays, cinema, contain many other famous examples of mentors and guides: Gandalf, Obi-Wan Kenobi, Dumbledore, Morpheus, Professor Xavier . . . the list goes on. Mentoring has even become a buzzword in business and education circles. Hundreds of websites are devoted to helping present and future business leaders understand the principles of sound mentoring. Entire graduate programs in education are built around mentoring and supervision for young teachers and professors.

But mentors are not the only types of relationships God uses to breathe courage into us. Often, the friends and companions He sends into our lives can provide strength, encouragement, and help for the journey. Ecclesiastes 4:12 captures the importance of friends when it says, "Though one may be overpowered, two can defend themselves. A cord of three strands is not quickly broken." We are always stronger in combination than we are in isolation, aren't we?

God knows this, and that is why He often equips us with helpers. In fact, one of the first things God did at creation was to make a suitable companion for Adam. In Genesis 2:18, God says, "It is not good for the man to be alone. I will make a helper suitable for him." And God made Eve.

I know for a fact I would be dead in the water without my wife. With her love, help, and understanding (*especially* her understanding), I have been able to continue moving forward.

You have no idea how many times I've lain in bed, paralyzed by fear. You have no idea how many times Brandi has grabbed my hand to say a quick prayer or looked me in the eyes to speak an encouraging word.

I pray each day for the wisdom and perception to aid her in her journey, too.

Confirmation Through Opportunity

Another way God confirms our dreams is through the opportunities He sends our way. Often, these are disguised as something we call coincidences. As Albert Einstein said, "Coincidence is God's way of remaining anonymous."

In his book *When GOD Winks: How the Power of Coincidence Guides Your Life,* SQuire Rushnell presents the idea that these seemingly random events can actually provide clues and assistance for making your way successfully through life. He sees coincidence as a spiritual "nudge" that helps us move in the direction we are meant to take.

Of course, as a Christian, I'm more inclined to see God's grace where other people see coincidence. I believe that when God has us embark on an adventure, He will not let us flounder without guidance. One of the last things Jesus said to His followers bears this out.

Just before His triumphant return to heaven, Jesus sent His disciples out on the great adventure of taking His name to the whole world with these words:

Go and make disciples of all nations, baptizing them in the name of the Father and of the Son and of the Holy Spirit, and teaching them to obey everything I have commanded you. And surely I am with you always, to the very end of the age. (Matthew 28:19–20)

Almost the last thing He said to His disciples while He was with them on the earth was, "I am with you always." No matter where they would go in their heroic quest to teach everyone about their Lord, His followers knew they would never be alone.

God will never leave *us* alone. And one of the ways He reminds us of this is when He sends little packages of grace—coincidences, if you want to call them that—to nudge us toward the path He wants us to walk.

Confirmation Through the Unexpected

Closely related to the surprising opportunities God sends us is the way He sometimes confirms our direction through unexpected circumstances or events. Actually, just about every great deliverance God has ever brought about for His people has been unexpected in some sense. What were the odds that a fifteen-year-old farm boy named David would go up against a nine-foot-tall trained Philistine killer and win? Who would have expected that three Hebrew youths tossed into a blazing furnace would come out alive—not even singed? And—the greatest surprise of all—how is it possible that a homeless rabbi who claimed to be the Messiah could be nailed to a Roman cross, completely bled out, buried in a tomb, and then alive again after three days?

Throughout the ages, God's faithful people have witnessed, again and again, how He snatches victory from the jaws of defeat, how He uses the weak to overcome the strong, how He produces life when no one else can see anything but death in the landscape. God specializes in the unexpected. He's practically in the flying pig business. So, why would you assume He wouldn't do that for you, too?

Our biggest problem with God's unexpected confirmations, as we've already discussed, is that we usually don't hang around long enough to see them happen. I get focused on my own schedules, my own resources, and my own perceptions, and I completely forget that God has His own calendar. He is doing things I can't comprehend. Why do I so often insist on limiting Him to my way of seeing?

One my heroes is George Mueller. He moved from Germany to England in 1829, and, within a few years, became convicted of the dire need for schools to provide basic education for the poor children and adults of Bristol, where he lived. By 1835, he had established five schools, though receiving no government support. Mueller believed that God would provide for his needs, and he never asked a single person for a donation.

Despite this, his religious educational organization received and disbursed £1,381,171—the equivalent of just over $151 million in today's dollars—in unsolicited gifts. The foundation he started to provide shelter and opportunity for orphans is still in operation today, providing care and education for children who would otherwise be on the street—or worse. And the organization continues its founder's methods. Actively shunning fundraising activities, the George Mueller Charitable Trust uses prayer as its sole means of sustenance.

If there's a Guinness world record for the number of coincidences experienced in a lifetime, George Mueller has got to be close to the top of the list. You see, he believed that instead of asking people for what he needed, he should only ask God. And God came through, time after time.

One morning, Mueller and his family sat down to breakfast with the orphans in the home although there was no food in the building. Nevertheless, Mueller offered thanks for the meal, and as he said "Amen," there was a knock on the door. It was a local baker, stopping by with enough fresh bread to feed all the children. By "coincidence," that same morning, the milkman's cart broke down in front of the orphanage, so he brought his load inside so everyone had fresh milk to drink.

In August 1877, Mueller was on board the SS *Sardinian*, bound for Canada. The ship encountered a thick fog bank, and the captain prudently slowed the ship for safety. Mueller, however, had an important appointment at his destination, and at the ship's present speed, he knew he would be late. He explained this to the captain, who was not a particularly religious man. The captain informed Mueller that it would be unsafe to make faster headway through the fog and that his appointment would simply have to be missed. Mueller then requested the use of the ship's chartroom to pray for the lifting of the fog. The captain agreed but told Mueller he was wasting his time.

Perhaps out of mere curiosity, however, the captain accompanied Mueller to the chartroom. After Mueller finished praying, the captain, for whatever reason, started to pray, but Mueller stopped him, informing him that the fog had already lifted.

They went back to the bridge, looked out, and saw the stars twinkling in the sky. The ship made port in time for Mueller's appointment, and not long after, the captain, a man named Joseph E. Dutton, became a Christian. In later years, he would come to be called "Holy Joe."

George Mueller lived his life expecting the unexpected. He didn't consider his experiences as coincidences. Instead, he fully expected God to answer his prayers.

Failures and Challenges

But not all of us have the same experience as George Mueller, do we? Sometimes, no matter how much we pray, the results we hope for do not materialize. Sometimes, when the unexpected happens, it seems like the end of the world. You've been there before. Maybe you're there right now. You cry out to God night after night but still nothing. You've started to wonder . . .

Does God know?

Does God care?

Joni Eareckson Tada was an active kid. She loved horseback riding, tennis, hiking, and swimming. One day in 1967, Joni was supposed to go play tennis with a friend, but for some reason the friend didn't show up. So, she decided at the last minute to go swimming with her sister in nearby Chesapeake Bay.

Joni misjudged the depth of the water when she dove in headfirst, and she fractured her cervical vertebrae. At the age of seventeen, she became a quadriplegic, with no movement from the shoulders down.

Joni says that during her two years of rehab, she experienced deep depression, rage, disbelief in God, and suicidal desires. But somehow, she persisted. She learned to paint by holding a brush in her teeth and actually began to experience success as an artist. She started writing about her experiences, and eventually she came to see her situation as a chance to advocate for disabled people.

To date, Joni Eareckson Tada has written some forty-eight books, has recorded six albums, and has even starred in a feature film about her life. Joni has reached the point where she can view her crippling accident as the point in her life where God began to truly use her powerfully.

Joni is a powerful testament to what can happen when someone allows God to transform tragedy into triumph. Through her organization, Joni and Friends, she reaches people worldwide with the message of hope, even in the midst of unimaginable difficulty.

Joni has been able to accept the type of unexpected event none of us would want to see as a chance for God to do something great, and she has received confirmation of her purpose. She personifies what Paul said in 2 Corinthians 12:9: "Therefore I will boast all the more gladly about my weaknesses, so that Christ's power may rest on me."

It may be that not many of us have the type of faith that is willing to see paralysis as an opportunity for God. There have not been many Joni Eareckson Tadas in the world and not many George Muellers, but I believe that, no matter what type of defeats you have experienced in your life or what type of challenge you are facing, God has the power to create blessing in it. We may not be able to see it now—or ever. But in the grand scheme of eternity, God will have the victory in our lives.

Taking the Exit Ramp

The final thing I want to say about expecting confirmation in the pursuit of the life that God has for us is that, sometimes, God shows us when it is time to step off the path. As Ecclesiastes 3 reminds us, there is a time and a season for every purpose in our lives. There is "a time to search, and a time to give up" (Ecclesiastes 3:6).

I've heard musicians say that the ideal time to end a performance is when you can leave them wanting just one more song. The worst time, of course, is when they've heard one tune too many, and they are looking at their watches and starting for the exits (there may be a lesson here for pastors, as well). It's all about timing. In other words, part of the art of living in holy rhythm is to know when God is showing you the exit ramp.

There is almost nothing sadder than to see someone we have admired—a great athlete, perhaps—who doesn't know when it is time to move on to the next phase of life. It can be downright painful to watch someone whose abilities have declined past the point of making a meaningful contribution, and he or she seems to be the only one who doesn't know it. The trouble is, they probably do know it, on some level, but they aren't willing to listen to that prompting from God in their heart of hearts, telling them it's time to move on.

I have a friend who was in ministry for many years who described for me the moment he realized God was giving him permission to lay down the burden. He had been laboring for years at a particular church. He was loved and appreciated, and no one really wanted him to go. And yet, he told me, God spoke clearly to his heart and let him know it was time. He had done his best for many years, and it was now time to step aside and give someone else an opportunity.

He did, and God blessed that season of his life and ministry. He left the church as a beloved senior pastor who was able to ease the transition and provide a blessing to the younger minister who took his place.

I realize that everyone's situation is different. It requires deep confidence in God and His leading to clearly perceive when it is time to stay on the road and when it is time to take the exit ramp. But I do believe God sometimes directs His faithful servants to a season of rest at the end of a task. And receiving that rest with grace and thankfulness—as a reward, not as a sign of failure—is the act of an obedient and trusting heart.

There is no question that beginning in faith and trust is very important. But *ending* the same way is just as important.

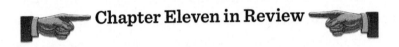

Chapter Eleven in Review

Key Ideas

1. God never calls any of His children to a task without providing for their needs.
2. Joshua anticipated confirmation of his obedience to the destiny God had planned for him and his people.
3. God provides confirmation through relationships.
4. God confirms our dreams through the opportunities He sends our way.
5. God sometimes confirms our direction through unexpected circumstances or events.
6. In the grand scheme of eternity, God will have the victory in our lives.
7. Ending well is just as important as beginning well.

Reflection Questions

1. Have you or someone you know ever had a "coincidence" that turned out to be very important in your life? What did you learn from the experience?

2. Can you think of a time when you "stopped walking before you got to the Jordan River"? If you could relive that situation, what would you do differently?
3. What are the main relationships in your life that give you strength? How do these relationships enable you to do what you need to do?
4. What keeps us from taking advantage of the opportunities that arise in our lives? What opportunities are you facing right now?
5. Are you considering the exit ramp in an area of your life? How do you know when it is time to recognize the ending of an effort or a phase of life?

Your Next Step

Think of an event in your life that represents to you a time of failure. Try to make a list of three things that resulted from the event that have borne positive fruit in the time since. Write a letter to your future self about the benefits that resulted from the failure.

TWELVE

PASS IT ON

*"When he ascended on high, he took many
captives and gave gifts to his people."*
—Ephesians 4:8

Often, when a hero completes the journey by returning to the "ordinary" world from the land of adventure, he brings with him gifts and blessings for those who receive him back. That is why, when Luke Skywalker has faced his deepest fears and overcome his most terrible enemies, he helps bring about peace in the galaxy. When Jason and his Argonauts return from their perilous voyage, they bring the Golden Fleece to King Pelias. When Samson finally realizes his strength came from God and not from himself, he helps bring about the downfall of the Philistines, the enemies of God's people. And, of course, when Jesus Christ triumphed over death, He bestowed the abiding presence of God, in the Person of the Holy Spirit, in the hearts of all those who remained faithful to Him.

It's pretty clear that those who achieve their dreams acquire a responsibility to others. Your accomplishment is not just about you and what you've done; it has implications for everyone you meet. God has not granted you the desires of your heart so you can sit back and relax. He desires for you to take up what you have learned and help His other children achieve the dreams He has given them.

Making the Handoff

Remember the old camp song, "Pass It On"? I often walk around our church office singing old camp songs or vacation Bible school songs and the staff looks at me like I'm crazy. When you have a really young staff as we do, more often than not, they've never even heard them. Either way, the lyrics to this song went like this:

> It only takes a spark to get a fire going;
> And soon all those around can warm up in its glowing.
> That's how it is with God's love,
> once you've experienced it;
> you spread His love to everyone,
> You want to pass it on.[1]

God's desire is that we should pass on, not only His love, but also the blessings and wisdom that come to us from making the journey of adventure, the pilgrimage toward our dreams. He does not sustain us and give us victory solely for our own good. He also intends the good of others.

Think about it: What if Louis Pasteur had discovered the vaccine for smallpox, and then kept the news to himself? What if Eli Whitney had invented the cotton gin just so he could use it on his own farm? Do you think Thomas Edison wanted to create a working light bulb just so he could use it in his own house?

The thing we admire most about our greatest heroes is the way their victories lead to victories for others. Martin Luther King Jr.'s moral and ethical leadership in the struggle for civil rights helped bring about better lives for millions of minority individuals. When Roger Banister broke the four-minute-mile barrier in 1954, he paved the way for future athletes to post faster and faster times.

No victory or accomplishment achieved with God's help is private property. It is meant to be shared.

The Greatest Lesson

In the Gospel of John, just before His arrest, mock trial, and crucifixion, Jesus provides an indelible example of how the greatest heroes fulfill their responsibility to give to others the gifts they have obtained during the journey. The first verse of John 13 tells us that Jesus was fully aware His time had come. He was quickly approaching the exit ramp and was about to complete God's dream of restoration for fallen humanity. But first, Jesus needed to teach His inner circle of followers a very important lesson. He was about to show them the full extent of His love. Very significantly, a couple of verses later, we read that Jesus "knew that the Father had put all things under his power, and that he had come from God and was returning to God" (John 13:3).

Pause and ask yourself the question: What would you do if you knew God had already given you the victory—that "all things were under your power"? How would you act?

I don't know about you, but I'm afraid I might be tempted to be a little too proud of myself. I might even be inclined to let the people around me know how lucky they were to get to hang out with me, but Jesus doesn't do anything like that. In fact, He goes to the opposite end of the spectrum. Instead of announcing to His followers His position at the top of the heap, He does something you would never expect of one who had just received "all power": He acts like a slave. John 13 records the dramatic scene:

> So he got up from the meal, took off his outer clothing, and wrapped a towel around his waist. After that, he poured water into a basin and began to wash his disciples' feet, drying them with the towel that was wrapped around him. (vv. 4–5)

To get the full impact of what Jesus is doing, you need to understand that foot washing was a task reserved for the lowliest slave in the household. Why? Well, think about it: people in this part of the world during this time in history walked around—wearing sandals, usually—on unpaved streets, in a time when there was little to no indoor or underground plumbing. The feet were generally considered the least honorable part of the body, mainly because they were in a perpetual state of uncleanness. So, although one was obliged to provide foot washing services for one's guests—especially at mealtimes—the job was given to the low servant on the totem pole, not the chief butler—and certainly not to the head of the household!

We can see this in Peter's reaction to the sight of his rabbi and teacher washing feet. John 13:6 says that when Jesus got around to Peter, the big, rough fisherman said, "Lord, are you going to wash my feet?"

Jesus answered Peter, "You do not realize now what I am doing, but later you will understand."

Clearly Peter still does not get it. "No," he says, "you shall never wash my feet."

Jesus' next words stop Peter in his tracks: "Unless I wash you, you have no part in me."

Peter's response is both heartwarming and amusing, if you understand his personality: "Then, Lord, not just my feet but my hands and my head as well!" (from verese 7–9).

Why is Peter initially so resistant to Jesus' actions? It is because he is shocked by the notion that this man whom he has come to admire so deeply would stoop to the dirtiest task of the lowest slave in the household. And yet, Jesus, as our Hero, is teaching us the greatest lesson love has to offer: the one who is greatest must serve the one who is least. Or, as Jesus Himself said in Mark 10:45, "For even the Son of Man did not come to be served, but to serve, and to give his life as a ransom for many."

Gifts of a Real Hero

The point here is not that Jesus became something less by offering Himself in humble service to those He loved. It is actually the opposite: If Jesus, who knew that all things were being placed in subjection to Him, could then turn in humility to teach His disciples the true meaning of love, how can anyone who claims to follow Him do otherwise?

Just as Max Lucado's older brother was the pathfinder through the tunnel, he was also the gift-giver: he brought the good news that the tunnel was safe. Jesus did not become *less* by serving and teaching His followers as He did—He became *more*!

In the same way, those of us who are pursuing the lives God has given us have the blessing and opportunity to display God's nature when we offer ourselves and what we have learned to others. We do not become less; we become more. I've noticed an interesting thing about the gifts that come from God: when they are given away freely, they tend to be multiplied back to the giver.

You've probably noticed this, too. Take love, for example. It isn't like a pie, where you have only so many slices before it's all gone. Instead, love just grows more and more, the more of it you give to others. It's like that magic pan of gingerbread in the old fairy tale: every day we can eat from it until we are full, and every morning, the pan is still full!

I can think of other examples: mercy, grace, forgiveness, loyalty, joy—in fact, almost everything that really matters in life and makes it worth living. Every time you give these great gifts away to someone else, you get back more than you gave. Jesus, our great Hero—the One who pursued God's plan all the way to the end and achieved it in a way no one else ever will—taught us, once and for all, that the more you empty yourself in God's name for the benefit of others, the more you will be filled.

I don't know about you, but that's a notion I don't think I'll ever get my head all the way around, even if I think about it for the rest of my time on earth. In fact, maybe it's better not to think about it too much; maybe it's better just to live it!

 Chapter Twelve in Review

Key Ideas

1. God does not sustain us and give us victory solely for our own good. He also intends it for the good of others.
2. The thing we admire most about our greatest heroes is the way their victories lead to victories for others.
3. Even the Son of Man did not come to be served, but to serve, and to give His life as a ransom for many.
4. The more you empty yourself in God's name for the benefit of others, the more you will be filled.

Reflection Questions

1. Think of some things you have learned from the people you admire. How have these gifts aided you on your own journey?

2. What do you think would happen if you tried to keep to yourself the lessons you have learned in your journey? Would you be more contented or less contented?

3. How can we share what we have learned without appearing arrogant?

4. How is humility related to the hero's gift-sharing?

Your Next Step

Is there someone in your circle of friends or acquaintances who seems to need some assistance or insight for the journey? Commit to praying for thirty days that God might show you an opportunity to be helpful. See what happens.

CONCLUSION

WASTE NOTHING

"Instructions for living a life. Pay attention.
Be astonished. Tell about it."
—Mary Oliver

When God had finished making the universe, He sat back and looked at what He had done. Then He said, "It is very good."

He made it just as He intended it. Nothing was wasted; nothing was out of place. It was perfect.

I realize that not long after, according to the Bible, sin came along and messed up God's original intentions for the universe. Humans, aided and abetted by the devil, allowed their own pride and self-will to spoil the perfect relationship God had with His creation. But the principle still applies: nothing God has designed is wasted. This is true in our lives when we are pursuing God's will. Nothing—loss, discouragement, joy, victory, achievement, failure, illness, success—that we gain or experience during the journey is ever wasted. It all has a purpose. Everything becomes a stitch in the grand tapestry God is weaving throughout time and eternity. And you and I—our lives, our hopes, our dreams, our victories, and our defeats—are part of that grand design.

What to Keep and What to Release?

One thing I hope I've communicated in this book is that not everything that comes into our lives is meant to be a permanent part of it. Part of continuing our climb, as we've already seen, is knowing when to let go of something in order to take hold of something else.

This requires courage, doesn't it? Sometimes, it is supremely difficult to let go of a relationship, for example, when that relationship is no longer contributing toward our God-given destiny. It takes deep trust in God to accept that the person we have known has a purpose of their own that no longer lies parallel to ours.

The apostle Paul learned this difficult truth in the case of a young man named Mark who had been one of his protégés. He had suggested to his friend and partner in ministry, Barnabas, they make a return trip to the churches they had helped build on their previous missionary journey, to see how they were getting along. Barnabas wanted to take Mark (some people called him John) with them, but Paul didn't think that was a good idea.

Apparently, at some point in their previous journey, when they were passing through a part of what we now know as southern Turkey—then called Pamphylia—the young man had turned away from the journey. We don't know why John Mark did this. Maybe things were getting hot, as they often did for Paul and Barnabas, and he didn't feel up to the challenge. Maybe he disagreed with Paul about something. Maybe he ran into some old friends and decided to hang out with them for a while, instead of traveling with Paul and Barnabas. But for whatever reason, he "deserted them in Pamphylia and had not continued with them in the work" (Acts 15:38). Because of that, Paul didn't want to take him on the upcoming trip.

But Barnabas disagreed, and the disagreement escalated to the point that these two faithful servants of God realized they were not going to see eye-to-eye on the matter. Barnabas and John Mark left for Cyprus, where Barnabas was from, and Paul departed for Syria, taking with him a companion by the name of Silas.

I can imagine that Paul felt a fair amount of sadness as he watched Barnabas and John Mark getting on the boat for Cyprus. After all, he and Barnabas had been through a lot together, all in the pursuit of God's mission. And for much of that time, John Mark was right there with them. You don't easily forget friends like that.

It is probably significant that, later in life, Paul was reconciled with John Mark. While he is imprisoned for his faith, Paul writes a letter to the church in Colossae in which he says, "My fellow prisoner Aristarchus sends you his greetings, as does Mark, the cousin of Barnabas. (You have received instructions about him; if he comes to you, welcome him.)" (Colossians 4:10). In all likelihood, the "Mark" of this passage is the same as the "Mark, sometimes called John" referred to in Acts 15. Now, he is sharing in Paul's imprisonment in the name of Christ, and Paul instructs the faithful people in Colossae to greet the young man and take care of him if he shows up.

Yet, at a certain point in his journey, Paul has to let go of John Mark and also his good friend, Barnabas. He watches them leave, and then he and Silas continue on their way.

One important lesson we can learn from this is that letting go is not the same thing as discarding. We do not know God's plans for the people, things, and events that enter our lives. Just because they are not part of our journey any more does not mean they are not being used by God for His own purposes. Sometimes, trusting God means accepting that our paths must diverge from the people, places, and things that have become familiar to us. As we are willing to let go and continue trusting, we are enabled to continue our journey toward all that God wants us to become.

The Great Adventure

As I close this book, my wish and prayer for you is that you would take steps of trust along the path toward God's best for your life. If you are just beginning the journey, I pray you will be granted faith to face the fear that will try to blockade you. I pray you can step out of the boat and start walking toward Jesus.

If you are farther along the trail, I pray God will continue equipping you for the steepening path. I pray He will bring into your life the people, resources, and circumstances that will enable you to withstand doubt, opposition, and worry.

And if you have been blessed to receive as reality the passions God has placed in your heart, I pray you will know the rich joy of sharing that blessing with others. May your hard-earned wisdom, offered in humility, bless and empower others who are just beginning journeys of their own.

In whatever part of the journey you find yourself, I pray, above all, that God will continue to strengthen you in your faith. Continue to "lift up your eyes" to the One who is always watching, always caring, and always providing.

This is how you make the journey of a lifetime—the journey to God's purposes for your life, and the way to find peace while chasing your dreams.

ACKNOWLEDGMENTS

To Brandi . . . thanks for your constant love, friendship, and patience. Your belief in me allows me to chase after my dreams. I can't imagine sharing this journey with anyone but you!

To Jett, Gage, and Brewer . . . you boys have no idea how much you are teaching me these days. I'm having the time of my life watching you three grow up. Never forget that I love you with all of my heart.

To Ben Stroup . . . thanks for your huge investment in this book. You are a fantastic writer and you make me a better writer. Brainstorming this with you from inception was a blast.

To my Cross Point Church family . . . thank you for allowing me to serve you. I love that together we're creating a place where everyone's welcome, because we know nobody's perfect, but we still believe anything's possible.

To the Cross Point Staff team . . . twelve years later it's still an honor to wake up every day and work with such an awesome group. You inspire me daily to be a better person. I love each and every one of you to death.

To Shannon Litton . . . thanks for your wisdom and faith

not only in this book, but in me. Thanks for confronting and redeeming my desire to give up!

To my entire team at W Publishing Group . . . Matt Baugher, Joel Kneedler, Stephanie Newton, Nicole Pavlas, Kristi Smith, Caroline Green, Adria Haley, Carol Martin, Debbie Wickwire, Paula Major, and Meaghan Porter . . . thank you guys for believing in me and giving me this incredible platform to share this message.

To Candice Watkins and Liz Barnard . . . you guys are helpful in a thousand ways. You go above and beyond on a daily basis, and I couldn't do what I do without you! Thanks for showing up every day and making this fun.

NOTES

Chapter 2

1. http://www.nba.com/history/players/jordan_bio.html.
2. Ibid.
3. http://www.brainyquote.com/quotes/quotes/m/michaeljor 127660.html.
4. http://en.wikipedia.org/wiki/Oprah_Winfrey, accessed August 3, 2014; *Business Insider*, October 29, 2012, http://www.business insider.com/15-people-who-failed-before-becoming-famous -2012-10?op=1, accessed August 3, 2014; *Harvard Gazette*, May 30, 2013, http://news.harvard.edu/gazette/story/2013/05 /winfrey-failure-is-just-movement/, accessed August 3, 2014.
5. http://news.harvard.edu/gazette/story/2013/05/winfreys -commencement-address/.
6. http://stevenleemusic.tumblr.com/post/78670948678/dear-mr -hewson-aka-bono-thank-you-for-submitting.
7. William Congreve, "The Mourning Bride," http://www.phrases .org.uk/meanings/179300.html.
8. Brennan Manning, *Ruthless Trust: The Ragamuffin's Path to God* (New York, NY: HarperCollins, 2000), 5.
9. Max Lucado, *Just Like Jesus* (Nashville, TN: Thomas Nelson, 2013).
10. John Ortberg, *The Me I Want to Be: Becoming God's Best Version of You* (Grand Rapids, MI: Zondervan, 2009), 136.

Chapter 4

1. Brennan Manning, *Ruthless Trust: The Ragamuffin's Path to God* (New York, NY: HarperCollins, 2000), 117.
2. Ibid., 22.

Chapter 5

1. Henri Nouwen, "A Spirituality of Waiting" (audio recording). Available at http://www.athomewithgod.co.uk/Nouwen%20 A%20Spirituality%20of%20waiting-1.pdf. Accessed July 25, 2014.

Chapter 7

1. C. S. Lewis, *The Weight of Glory* (New York, NY: HarperCollins, 1949).
2. John Ortberg, "Kings and Priests," catalystspace.com.
3. Seth Godin, *The Dip: A Little Book that Teaches You When to Quit (and When to Stick)* (New York, NY: Portfolio, 2007).
4. Dionysius of Alexandria, "To the Brethren in Alexandria," http://www.gutenberg.org/files/36539/36539-h/36539-h.htm. Accessed July 13, 2014.
5. Emperor Julian, "To Arsacius, High-priest of Galatia," http://www.tertullian.org/fathers/julian_apostate_letters_1_trans .htm. Accessed July 13, 2014.
6. Viktor Frankl, *Man's Search for Meaning* (New York, NY: Pocket Books, 1972), 56–57.
7. Ibid.
8. Eleanor Roosevelt, http://www.goodreads.com/quotes/3823 -you-gain-strength-courage-and-confidence-by-every -experience-in.

Chapter 10

1. Corrie ten Boom, *Tramp for the Lord* (Fort Washington, PA: CLC Publications, 2011), 41.

2. J. R. R. Tolkien, *The Lord of the Rings* (Boston: Houghton Mifflin, 2001), 696.

Chapter 12
1. "Pass It On." http://www.higherpraise.com/lyrics1/7 PassItOn.htm. Copyright 1969, Bud John Songs, Inc. Words and music by Kurt Kaiser.

ABOUT THE AUTHOR

Photo by Lee Steffen

Pete Wilson is the founding and senior pastor of Cross Point Church in Nashville, Tennessee, a committed church community that he and his wife, Brandi, planted in 2002. Cross Point has grown to reach more than six thousand people each weekend through its seven campuses located around the Nashville area, and online. As one of the fastest-growing churches in America, Pete's ministry—an outreach focused on helping people become devoted to Christ, irrevocably committed to each other, and relentlessly dedicated to reaching those outside of God's family with the gospel—has made him a frequent speaker at national and international church conferences.

Pete gained national attention in 2010 when Thomas Nelson published his best-selling book, *Plan B*, a title that has been printed in five languages and launched *Putting Plan B into Action*, a 6-week DVD curriculum that serves as a study companion to the book. *Empty Promises*, Pete's second book, focuses on the human desire to find purpose and hope in things that are not God. By writing honestly and transparently, Pete looks to help the reader identify their own inclination to drift toward putting their identity in other things and offer them a wake-up call to find their meaning in Christ alone. *Let Hope In*, Pete's third book, presents a new look at the power of healing through hope, revealing four unique choices that have the potential to change your life forever. In Pete's fourth book, *What Keeps You Up At Night?*, his wish and prayer is that you would take steps of trust along the path toward God's best for your life; that you will be granted faith to face the fear that will try to blockade you; that you can step out of the boat and start walking toward Jesus; that He will bring into your life the people, resources, and circumstances that will enable you to withstand doubt, opposition, and worry.

Pete earned his bachelor's degree in communications from Kentucky Western University and attended seminary at Southern Seminary in Louisville, Kentucky. Pete is also an avid blogger (www.PeteWilson.tv); he enjoys the outdoors, farming, and Titans football. When he's looking for rest, you can often find Pete working in his garden, hanging out with Brandi, or playing outside with their three boys.

ALSO AVAILABLE FROM

PETE WILSON

AVAILABLE WHEREVER
BOOKS AND EBOOKS ARE SOLD

THOMAS NELSON
Since 1798

WHAT KEEPS YOUR
FRIENDS
UP AT NIGHT?

The *What Keeps You Up at Night?* Bible Study will help you dig deeper into the concepts covered in this book and share the message with your church or small group. The study includes six 15-minute teaching videos from Pete Wilson, questions for group discussion, additional activities for individual study, and more. Now you can replace your uncertainties with a practical plan to develop your faith. And you can help others dismantle the fears that steer them away from their God-given dreams.